Digital Video

Volume 2

A Collection of Papers on Digital Video Technology
Presented during Technical Conferences of the SMPTE
on 1 November 1978 and 3 February 1979

Edited by
M. Carlos Kennedy
Ampex Corporation, Redwood City, California

Published in March 1979 by the
Society of Motion Picture
and Television Engineers
862 Scarsdale Avenue
Scarsdale, New York 10583

Contents

Editor's Foreword

Developments in the field of digital video since our last publication two years ago have continued to exceed nearly everyone's forecast. It's no longer a question of when the broadcaster will use digital video devices, but rather what will be the next new digital video device that he will use.

The first digital video book concerned itself with more fundamental discussions. The reader is referred to the tutorial section of the first book for background information, and the glossary and bibliography for reference materials.

The papers collected in this book are intended to bring the broadcaster up to date on the latest progress of digital video technology. These papers have not been previously published, but were delivered at the most recent SMPTE Conferences in New York (1 November 1978) and San Francisco (3 February 1979).

Many advancements have been made in the application of digital video technology in the past two years. Experimental digital video recorders have been demonstrated by the Independent Broadcast Authority, in cooperation with Bosch-Fernseh, and by the Ampex Corporation. Digital technology has been employed in the production of graphic illustrations for television, as well as for computer animation. The resulting artwork is now being used in daily television broadcasting.

Teletext systems for broadcasting multiple pages of alphanumeric information are now in operation in Europe, and experimentation has started in the United States for similar systems. Digitally modulated optical laser systems are being used experimentally in place of the conventional ENG microwave systems.

Though many new systems have been developed, the all-digital television facility is still in the distant future. In recognition of the continued requirement for analog to digital converters, semiconductor manufacturers have designed and are producing integrated circuits for this purpose. Memory chips are increasing in their bit-storage capabilities at ever decreasing costs, making expanded digital television devices within the reach of all broadcasters.

Digital special-effects systems using frame synchronizers and time-base correctors continue to be developed with increasing numbers and varieties of effects, including multiple nonsynchronous inputs.

Research continues in the field of bit-rate reduction. The designer is faced with the problem of reducing hardware and tape costs for transmission and storage of the digital signal without any appreciable reduction in picture quality. The designer is also faced with the problem of multiple world television standards and whether component or composite signals should be used in the digital television system of the future. Digital television can be a means of easing the problems of program interchange in the world standards.

All of the above subjects are covered by the papers published in this book and give the reader further insight into the latest techniques and application of digital technology and equipment. We hope this book will continue to expand your knowledge in the exciting field of digital video.

M. Carlos Kennedy
Redwood City, California
7 February 1979

Advertisers' Index

The ANTIOPE Broadcast Teletext System

Yves Guinet
CCETT
Rennes, France

INTRODUCTION

The ANTIOPE system was conceived in 1973 and studied at the CCETT public telecommunications and broadcasting communications research center in Rennes since that time. Its first public demonstration in France was conducted by TDF in September of 1976. Since this time regular experimental transmissions have been made.

Teletext constitutes a primary example of a broadcast system that is completely digital, from the source to the receiver. Such results are due to both the advanced technology in generating alphanumeric or graphic color displays on TV screens and the improvements in the broadband transmission of data.

This paper is not intended as a detailed technical description of ANTIOPE, but rather as a definition of the main concepts of the global system.

A PAGE OF TELETEXT

A current examination of the sources for a teletext message on a TV screen, from the user's point of view, must distinguish between the local and remote sources.

In relation to the remote sources, a broadband distribution channel can be used which provides access to the message through a simple selective procedure. In this class, we will find radio transmission by VHF or UHF as well as the use of cable or satellite as a connecting link. Explaining this is one major subject of this paper.

The text message on the screen can be associated with a normal TV program or an aural radio transmission. It can also constitute a new form of service via broadband distribution network for entirely new audiences (Fig. 1).

In 1972, these were the only applications, but it became rapidly evident that a second potential, using the telephone local loop as the narrow-band interactive channel, was also possible.

Rapid access, on individual demand, to a distant data base, which is organized in page form, greatly enlarged the initial concept. The concurrent development of new interactive data networks such as "packet switching network" made possible this second category of applications.

An entry function, permitting an easy screen composition, appeared to be a key factor. Availability of vast data bases arranged in page format will necessitate a large amount of editing and updating from greatly decentralized input points.

The question of message exchanges between data bases in the international sphere presupposes operational standards that permit conversion of alphabets or transmission codes. Obviously, local memory for storage is needed to assist in the set-up or editing function. However, these memories will also be used to complement or support the transmission function both in one-way and two-way applications.

In fact, it is clear today that the future of teletext requires a good compatibility between those different applications, especially in view of their interdependencies. This is the direction of the common recommendations of CCIR and CCITT and the reason for their common new working group on this subject.

It would appear that first-generation of broadcast teletext systems have certain limits which do not permit full compatibility. Two basic principles in these systems create these restrictions, and they are:
(1). Writing a page of text by rows with a fixed length block of codes.
(2). Locking this fixed length block to the horizontal line rate of the TV signal. This second principle makes application of the system to a 4.2 MHz NTSC signal format more difficult.

In the ANTIOPE system we have separated these two categories of problems and have designed what we consider to be a more flexible system.

VISUALISATION AND TRANSMISSION

The essential characteristic of ANTIOPE is to separate the aspect of data entry and display from the various methods of transmission available.

For data entry and display, the dominant factors are human dexterity, visual recognition and even sociological aspects such as linguistics.

The visual matrix having been defined (e.g., 40 lines of 25 characters), it is required that the alphanumeric characters cover the full language they are assigned to. This requirement was initially underestimated, but the need for international exchange and the diversity of languages to be covered has rapidly brought this question to the fore.

It is also important that the graphic capabilities of the system enjoy the full range of color and form that maximum exploitation renders.

At this level, the manual composition of updating of a page of teletext is the most important consideration: it should be possible to colorize geographic charts out of standard archives, without any limitations beyond those imposed by the matrix, while enjoying the full choice of colors and graphic symbols. Fixed system formats introduce at this level some considerable constraints.

These diverse considerations led us to represent the page on the display or at the keyboard, by a 16-bit code language, each code describing the character at a given location on the visual matrix.

At the level of the transmitting system, the dominant factors are of a totally different nature. First, it is necessary to take into account the existing ISO and CCITT standards for text communications. For this reason, the ASCII sets of codes must be kept as a basis for the definition of the transmission languages. Second, it is necessary to take into account the properties of the various transmission media. A broadcasting system does not have the same properties as a cable or a point-to-point narrow-band transmission system. We must admit that the sequence of codes to broadcast a page will not be exactly the same as the sequence to transmit or store it (Fig. 2).

8

However, two considerations limit the possible differences:
(1). It should be possible to convert the codes of one language to those of another, without any disturbance or alteration of the message at the display level.
(2). It should cost as little as possible to make this translation.

The CCIR and CCITT specially created a common working group to establish this compatibility, and it is the main concept of ANTIOPE as a language to try to ensure it.

THE STRUCTURE AND FUNCTIONS OF THE TERMINAL

The ANTIOPE terminal is directly based on the above principles. The following description deals only with the codes processing and display. The visual presentation in all applications is done with the 16-bit code language.

The network interfaces, however, work on 8-bit code language for both one-way and two-way applications. The code processing unit, which is a microprocessor, uses a general software to handle the compatible code processing. It converts the 8-bit codes data stream into the 16-bit codes for visual presentation (Fig. 3). In addition, it applies specific processing for each type of network: for broadcasting, it processes the code redundancy necessary to provide the message robustness.

THE TITAN INTERACTIVE SYSTEM

In telephone line applications for data base access, the French P.T.T. decided to use the ANTIOPE language within the framework of the Titan interactive system for interactive teletext. A half-duplex 1200-75-baud (1 byte/s) modem is used to interface the Titan terminal to the interactive network.

DIDON: THE BROADCAST STANDARD FOR PACKAGED DATA

For broadcasting teletext, through the TV channel, TDF uses the ANTIOPE language to feed a new TV compatible packet data broadcasting system called DIDON (Fig. 4).

The principles are the same as those used in the modern interactive networks as previously mentioned. This will open a wide range of new possibilities for the development of broadcast data systems.

The major objectives are as follows:
(1). No modification of the present existing TV channels, whatever they are.
(2). An easy adaptability to the variety of current international TV standards including varying channel bandwidths.
(3). Possibility to easily share the high bit rates (in the range of 3 Mbit/s) between a large number of independent applications. Packet data broadcasting gives an easy solution to this problem.
(4). To be transparent, which means at the level of the network not to have to know about any application, nor to impose any form of specific constraint to anyone.

The packet data broadcasting concept consists of making packets from the incoming data and of putting on each packet a prefix or header which will allow the handling of it in a completely autonomous way, for instance:
(1). To demodulate it, which means to get bit and byte synchronization.

(2). To know its origin by use of an address.
(3). To know if some packets are lost, thanks to a continuity index.
(4). To know the length of the block of data on the packet.

Such a system allows one to make use of the full capacity or of just part of the TV channel to transmit or broadcast data either alone or in the presence of the TV program (Fig. 5). The main application at the moment for the Didon system is to broadcast, but thanks to its inherent transparency, it will be possible to handle many other applications without any modification of the data standard. Numerous field test trials have been conducted in France and in Switzerland, and new methods allow one to measure error patterns at the receiving end.

The influences of noise, multipath propagation, bit frequency value, and demodulation techniques have been objectively evaluated in terms of error rates.

Statistical properties of errors have been studied, and we know today the diversity and the importance of the receiving conditions: to receive data in a town with a strong field and multipath propagation is completely different from reception in a mountainous country, with just a weak field.

CONCLUSION

ANTIOPE is clearly a global approach to teletext communication, giving to both one-way and two-way networks compatible and equal facilities. Experience alone will tell us which applications have to be implemented on this kind of network. It is clear that there is no evident reason for this arrangement to be the same from country to country.

Didon, on the other hand, is a new approach fro TV compatible high-capacity data broadcasting systems which will handle the ANTIOPE data codes. Broadcasting must have the necessary tools to face the development of digital technologies, either to improve the services for its present audience or to find new sorts of audiences.

ANTIOPE and Didon both open the way to written digital broadcasting.

BIBLIOGRAPHICAL REFERENCES

1. "Specification of Standards for Information Transmission by Digitally Coded Signal in the Field Blanking Interval of 625-line Television Systems," published simultaneously by the BBC, the IBA, and BREMA, Oct. 1974.

2. "Digital Information Service: British Standards for Domestic Data Broadcasting," E.B.U. Rev., 149: 11-17, Feb. 1975.

3. "Documents of C.C.I.R. Study Group 11. Period 1974-78:" "Broadcasting of Still Pictures and Other Information Intended for the Public and Using a Television Channel," Question 2, Question 29/11 (Rev. 76); "Standards for a New Broadcasting Service: Teletext," Study Programme 29B/11 (Rev. 76); "Specifiactions for Multiplex Broadcasting of Information in the Television Channel," Study Programme 29C/11; "Still-Image Broadcasting Using a Television Channel," Report AD/11.

4. Y. Guinet, "New Services Offered by a Packaged-Data Broadcasting System," E.B.U. Rev. 149: 3-10, Feb. 1975.

5.   Y. Noirel, "Un système expérimental de diffusion de données par paquets (An Experimental System for Broadcasting Data in Packets)," <u>Rev. Radiodiffusion-Télévision</u>, 40: 11-17, Nov./Dec. 1975.

6.   B. Marti, and M. Maudit, "ANTIOPE, service de télétext (ANTIOPE, teletext system)," <u>Rev. Radiodiffusion-Télévision</u>, 40: 18-23, Nov./Dec. 1975.

7.   C. Gautier, et al., "Epeos, service d'enregistrement automatique des programmes (Epeos, Automatic Program Recording System)."

8.   "First Public Demonstration of the ANTIOPE Teletext System," <u>E.B.U. Rev.</u>, 161: 41-42, Feb. 1977.

9.   C. Schwartz, et al., "Spécification préliminaire du système de télétext ANTIOPE (Preliminary Specification of the ANTIOPE Teletext System)," <u>Rev. Radiodiffusion-Télévision</u>, 47: 1-8, Apr./May 1977.

10.   B. Marti, "Problèmes linguistiques en radiodiffusion de l'ecrit (Linguistics Problems in Broadcasting Written Text)," Documents of the 10th International Television Symposium, Session D, Montreux, June 1977.

11.   Y. Guinet, "Comparative Study of Broadcast Teletext Systems: Some Advantages of the Application of Packaged Data Broadcasting to Teletext," <u>E.B.U. Rev.</u>, Tech. 165: Oct. 1977.

Yves Guinet is Deputy Director of the CCETT (TV and Telecommunications Research Center) responsible for research and development in fields of new technology that affect television broadcasting. He has been very active in the fields of teletext and digital video. He is a member of E.B.U. Sub-Group V2 on teletext and has published several papers on the ANTIOPE teletext system in the <u>E.B.U. Technical Review.</u> Currently, Mr. Guinet is serving as chairman of E.B.U. Sub-Group V1 on Digital Coding of Picture and Sound (formerly Working Party C).

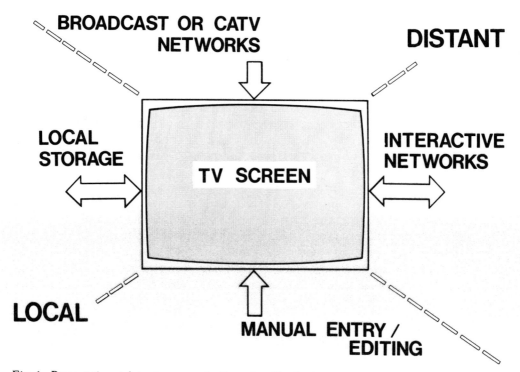

Fig. 1. Present-time teletext communications should take into account both distant and local data sources.

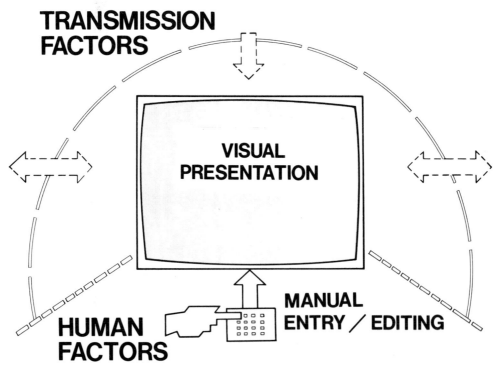

Fig. 2. The teletext system must distinguish the transmission factors (broadcast and interactive) from the human factors (display or entry).

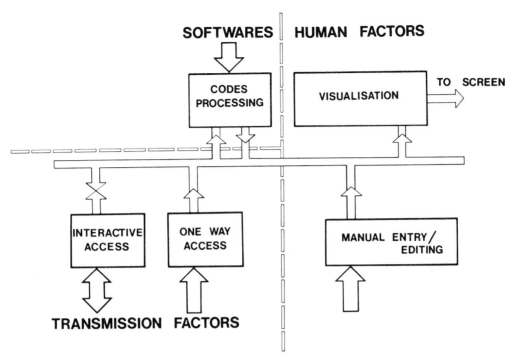

Fig. 3. In the compatible ANTIOPE teletext receivers, the microprocessor converts the 8-bit transmission code language into the 16-bit display code language.

DIDON

THE PACKET DATA TV BROADCASTING SYSTEM

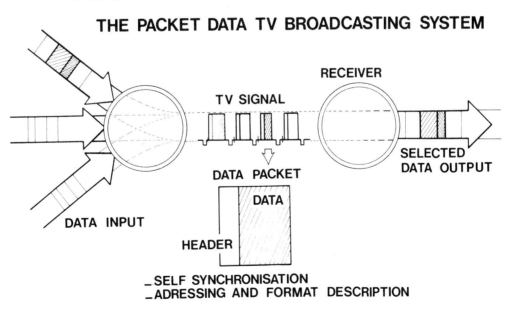

Fig. 4. The Didon packet data TV broadcast system introduces a completely new way to use the TV channel.

Fig. 5. The digital data transmitted by ANTIOPE is assigned to unused lines in the vertical interval, as seen in the expanded view above.

Optical Television Link Employing a Digitally Modulated Laser

A. A. Goldberg, S. Juchnowycz and J. Rossi
CBS Technology Center
Stamford, Connecticut

INTRODUCTION

Producers of news, sports and on-location drama television programs strive to make their shows more interesting and immediate. A technique that is becoming increasingly popular is to use a mobile television camera and micro-wave links to convey the picture and sound back to the control point. The limited number of microwave channels available for this purpose can be sup-plemented with optical links over unobstructed paths of a kilometer or less. FCC authorization is not required but the light beams must be safe in the environment.

The CBS Technology Center has built an experimental model of a digital laser link, which is shown in Fig. 1. It can carry one NTSC color television picture signal and two high-quality sound signals across a distance of one kilometer in clear air. The range is reduced in fog and rain. Pulse code modulation ensures that the quality of the signals remains high as long as the link operates above the threshold point, defined as a bit error rate (BER) of 10^{-7}. A bit serial digital code has been developed that is rela-tively simple and efficient for television purposes. A monochromatic light beam permits the use of a narrow bandpass optical filter in the receiver to remove most background interference. The power density of the beam is low enough to be environmentally safe with a few simple precautions. The range of the digital laser link can be increased by improving the collection efficiency of the receiving antenna.

OPTICAL LINK SYSTEM

Figure 2 is a simplified block diagram of the optical television link. It employs PCM intensity modulation with the bits coded as the presence or ab-sence of the light carrier. The laser current is varied in accordance with the bit stream. At the receiver the light carrier is collected, filtered by an optical pass filter and sensed by a photodetector. The resultant electrical signal is filtered to the information spectrum, which in this case is approximately 1 to 100 MHz. Finally, a decision is made as to whether the carrier plus noise signal exceeds a decision threshold during a bit period. Errors occur whenever the detected carrier plus noise does not exceed the threshold, given that the carrier is present. Errors will also occur when the threshold is exceeded by noise alone. This is graphically displayed with an eye pattern on the oscilloscope screen. Valid decisions can be made only if the pattern has open spaces (eyes) that are free of signals and noise.

OPTICAL CHANNEL

The optical transmission channel in the earth's atmosphere will be attenu-ated by the weather, air pollution, and sundry other influences. Absorp-tion in the lower atmosphere is due primarily to water vapor and carbon dioxide. Beam scattering can be caused by molecular-sized particles such as smoke and fog in the air. Figure 3 presents measurements of the atmo-spheric transmissivity as a function of wavelengths.[1]

The solid line represents both absorption and scattering. The dashed line shows how scattering alone varies with wavelength. Air turbulence due to thermal effects causes the beam to deviate from the line-of-sight path and to spread. All these factors reduce the amount of light that will impact the receiver. Transmissivity of the atmosphere increases with wavelength, except where absorptions exist. Another advantage of longer wavelengths is that the effects of air turbulence are reduced. Atmospheric windows I and II are the bands of interest for our purposes.

BACKGROUND RADIATION

The performance of the digital laser link can be influenced by the presence of background radiation from the sun, sky, and man-made lights. These will impair signal detection by increasing the detector shot noise level. In a PCM transmission system the output SNR is limited by the quantizing noise when operating above threshold (defined as BER of 10^{-7}). Because the BER is a function of the carrier-to-noise-power ratio at the detector, background radiation will add noise power and require a commensurate increase in signal power to maintain the BER constant. In effect, the range of the links will be reduced. However, the television picture remains unimpaired as long as the link operates above the threshold point, regardless of background radiation.

The spectrum of sunlight is extremely broad and peaks in the same region as the photodiode. Reception with the sun as a direct background is not feasible because of its high brightness. Specular reflections of the sun off water and shiny objects will also be intense. Another source of background radiation is the sky due to scattering of incident light. Clear skylight has a spectrum that peaks in the blue region but still has considerable power in the infrared. Radiances for sunlit clouds are considerably higher.

A great deal of the background radiation can be removed by an optical filter placed at the entrance of the receiver. The spectral response of the filter is bandpass, with a transmission peak at 820 nm and a bandwidth of 10 nm at 50% of peak. The insertion loss is 50%. The filter is seldom used and only when needed during operations with high background radiation. Most situations do not require a filter because the narrow acceptance angle of the receiver is sufficient to avoid interference.

LIGHT SOURCE

Light sources should be long-lived, efficient, inexpensive and preferably solid state. Response times in the order of a few nanoseconds are needed to convey digital modulation. Transfer functions can be non-linear because PCM requires only that the state of each bit be recognized. Output powers should be sufficient for the maximum operating distance but must not pose an environmental health hazard.

Two types of semiconductor light sources that can be used are light-emitting diodes (LEDs) and injection lasers. Ternary GaAlAs is the most commonly used semiconductor material, and the emission wavelengths range from 750 to 1065 nm.

LEDs emit radiation over a solid angle of 2π steradians so that the output power emitted into a unit solid angle per unit emission area is low. The spectral bandwidths of LEDs are broad, ranging from 25 to 40 nm. Stripe geometry edge emitter LEDs have low injection capacitances, which leads to a modulation bandwidth of 100 to 140 MHz. Modulation is accomplished by varying the injection current and is reasonably linear. LEDs are low in cost and have usable lifetimes of 5×10^5 hours. We elected not to use an LED in the optical link because of the difficulty of generating a sufficient power output in a collimated beam.

Semiconductor injection lasers radiate directionally but don't produce the pencil of light normally associated with lasers. About 40% of the radiant flux is contained within a cone half angle of 20°. The stripe geometry produces an elliptical cone of light with an axial ratio of roughly 3:1. As a result, it is relatively easy to collimate the beam for transmission. The spectral bandwidth of the injection laser is in the order of 4 nm. Modulation bandwidth exceeds 100 MHz but the transfer function is non-linear. Injection lasers emit substantial optical power for small changes in the driving current above threshold, as shown in the measured curve of Fig. 4. Threshold current is quite temperature dependent, so the injection laser must be temperature stabilized at about 20^OC.

An RCA C30130 aluminum gallium arsenide injection laser is used in the digital laser link. The output wavelength is 820 nm, which is in the near infrared region. Digital modulation is produced by an 80 mA (peak-to-peak) current superimposed on a direct current of 300 mA. It causes the optical output power density to swing between the lasing threshold of about 0.5 mW to a maximum of 6 mW. The modulation waveform has a 50% duty cycle, so the average output power is approximately 3.3 mW.

Cooling the laser is accomplished with a Peltier effect thermo-electric device in contact with the heat sink. Temperature is sensed by a thermistor, and a feedback signal controls a current amplifier to maintain the temperature constant.

PHOTODETECTORS

The photodetector used in the receiver should be chosen to generate the highest signal-to-noise ratio (SNR) at the output signal. It involves collecting the maximum light flux on the target area and choosing a detector with the lowest noise equivalent power (NEP) and the highest quantum efficiency. Of course, an important consideration is that the spectral response of the detector must accept the wavelength of the light source.

Two types of solid-state photoconductors have the required short response times in the order of a few nanoseconds. They are the PIN photodiode and the avalanche photodiode (APD). Table I is a comparison of detector types.[2] An APD was chosen for the optical link because of its larger target area and much higher responsivity, which is the average emitted current divided by the average incident power. Also, the total NEP of an APD is lower than that of the PIN photodetector. A disadvantage of the APDs is that they must operate at a high bias voltage (275 V) and require a close control of current and voltage. Spectral response peaks very broadly between 700 and 950. An RCA C30884 photodetector is used in the digital laser link.

OPTICAL ANTENNAS

The optical antennas in the link employ refractive lenses for collimating and collecting. Imaging per se is not required. The basic transmission-reception geometry is shown in Fig. 5. Light from the transmitter is sent with a beam spread angle θ radians. At a distance R at the plane of the receiver, the area covered by the beam is:

$$\frac{\pi(\theta R)^2}{4}$$

The receiving antenna with a diameter of d will intercept an area of:

$$\frac{\pi d^2}{4}$$

Transmitter pointing error angle, $\mathcal{E}$, should be less than

$$\frac{\theta}{2} - \text{arc } \tan\left(\frac{d}{2R}\right)$$

in order for the beam to illuminate the receiving antenna.

The transmitting antenna in the digital laser television link is a plano-convex Fresnel type plastic lens, 10 cm in diameter and with a focal length of approximately 25 cm. About 20% of the total output flux of the laser is collimated by the lens. The beam spread angle θ is about 1 milliradian, making the receiver plane area 1 km away about 0.8 m^2, or a circle 1 m in diameter. Transmitter pointing error $\mathcal{E}$ must be within ½ milliradian.

The receiving antenna consists of a plano-convex Fresnel type plastic lens with a useful diameter of 25 cm and a secondary relay lens. The receiving antenna area is 0.05 m^2. Thus, only 6.25% of the transmitted flux can be collected by the receiver. This is an approximation because the intensity of the beam is maximum on its center axis and falls off toward its periphery. Therefore, an error in pointing will result in less received power and a reduction in the threshold range.

SERIAL DIGITAL CODE

Digital television circuits in broadcasting plants are presently configured bit-parallel because the codecs process parallel bit streams and parallel memories can employ slow speed logic elements. The bit rate of each B parallel circuit is equal to the sampling rate, F_s, which is usually three or four times the 3.58 MHz color subcarrier, F_{sc}. The digital laser link, however, requires a bit-serial stream in order to be carried on the single transmission channel. The serial code described here can also be used in a digital radio link and in a television plant. Long-distance transmission of digital television signals will require bit reduction circuits to be cost effective and is not addressed here.

Pulse code modulation (PCM) with linear binary coding is usually used for television picture signals. The laser link employs a sampling rate of $3F_{sc}$, but can readily be converted to $4F_{sc}$ when it becomes the recommended practice.[3]

Good quality color NTSC pictures require that each video sample be quantized to 8 bit accuracy (B=8).[4] Therefore, the bit rate of the digital signal is $B \times F_s$, or approximately 86Mbits.

Later, we shall see that ancillary signals can be carried without an increase in the total bit rate. It is accomplished by inserting these bit streams into inactive periods of the television lines and fields.

No attempt has been made to reduce the bit rate by not transmitting during the horizontal and vertical blanking periods. Audio and digital synchronizing information, however, is carried during H blanking. To save the V blanking time will require a 20H memory at the sending end and another at the receiving end. We prefer to avoid this circuit complexity.

Baseband Digital Code

The choice of a baseband digital code is influenced by a number of factors:
(a). Bit and codeword timing information must be capable of being extracted from the digital stream.
(b). ac coupled circuits with poor low-frequency response and a null at dc are readily realized at low cost. These can be used when long strings of symbols of one polarity are not present in the code.
(c). As the code is designed specifically for television signals, full use can be made of the baseband video signal characteristics.
(d). Channel bandwidth utilization must be high, i.e., many bits per hertz should be carried in a channel.
(e). A two-signal state code is required.

A non-return-to-zero (NRZ) code is preferred because it yields the smallest probability of error for a given energy per bit of any baseband coding scheme. Figure 6 shows a unipolar NRZ with "0" at the lower level and "1" at the upper level. Notice that whenever a long string of "0's" or "1's" occurs, the level remains constant and represents a large low frequency component. The power spectrum envelope of the NRZ code is shown in Fig. 7. Most of the energy is located below the frequency $1/T$, where T = the bit period. For the 86Mbits digital TV signal, T = 11.6 ns and $1/T$ = 86 MHz. Another problem with an NRZ code is the difficulty of extracting clock synchronizing information during long strings of any one symbol. The NRZ code has high energy at low frequencies and requires circuits with dc response. Also, it is difficult to synchronize the bit clock at the receiver. These problems can be avoided with a baseband code called "reverse alternating codeword, non return to zero" (RAC-NRZ).

The analog NTSC composite television signal is converted to PCM, sampled at $3F_{sc}$ = 10.7 MHz, 8 bits per codeword, in bit-parallel form. During the process of converting to bit-serial form, every other 8-bit codeword is complemented; that is, "0" becomes "1" and vice versa. It is interesting to note that the dc component of the bit-serial stream becomes constant regardless of the content of the television signal. This is true as long as the PCM sampling rate exceeds the Nyquist sampling limit.[5]

Figure 8 is the low-frequency spectrum of an NRZ bit-serial, PCM television composite signal with blanking only. Note the high energy at zero frequency and at the encoding frequency of 10.7 MHz. Figure 9 is the spectrum from 0 to 100 MHz of the same NRZ stream. The high peaks are the 10.7 MHz sampling rate and its harmonics.

When the reverse alternating codeword feature is used (RAC-NRZ), the spectrum changes to that shown in Fig. 10. The energy is minimal at zero frequency and peaks at 5.35 MHz, which is one-half the sampling frequency. Figure 11 shows the spectrum of the RAC-NRZ signal from 0 to 100 MHz. Note the high energy peaks at 5.35 MHz and its odd harmonics.

Both Figs. 9 and 10 show an energy peak at the bit rate of 86 MHz. Conceivably, these can be used to synchronize a bit clock generator in the receiver.

The block diagram of a basic RAC-NRZ transmission system is shown in Fig. 12. At the sending terminal, there are an ADC to generate a bit-parallel digital television signal, a parallel-to-serial converter, and an RAC coder. At the receiving terminal, there are an RAC decoder, a serial-to-parallel converter, and a DAC. In a practical circuit, the parallel-to-serial converter and the RAC coder are combined; likewise, the RAC decoder and the serial-to-parallel converter in the receiving terminal.

Synchronization

In order to reconstruct the bit-parallel digital television signal at the receiving terminal, it is necessary to separate the codewords, establish their polarity, and clock the individual bits. These functions are word sync, word polarity, and bit clock, respectively. All three are available during the H sync pulse.

At the leading edge of the television signal's H sync pulse, a start-of-sync signal is forced to be generated, consisting of three words, all "0." This is unique because the RAC-NRZ stream will not permit a string of 24 zeros in a row. It is followed by approximately 50 words of alternating polarity, which causes the bit-serial code to be eight "1's," eight "0's," eight "1's," etc. This results in a strong 5.35 MHz component that provides word sync and word polarity information. An end-of-sync signal consisting of three words, all "1," is generated at the trailing edge of the H sync pulse. It is used to terminate the digital synchronization functions and to initiate the digital audio signals. Figure 13 shows where these digital signals are located relative to the analog television signal.

Bit clock can be constructed in one of two ways: (a). multiply the previously mentioned 5.35 MHz component by 16 to produce 86 MHz, or (b). synchronize a phase-locked loop oscillator to the 86 MHz energy in the serial bit stream. The laser link employs a variation of the former method.

Audio

Two digital audio signals totalling 64 bits are carried in the breezeway of the television signal. As shown in Fig. 14, each sound channel is PCM encoded at a $2F_h$ rate, with 14 bits per sample. The encoding rate of 31.5 kHz permits the audio frequency response to exceed 12 kHz, which is sufficient for television purposes. Two parity bits can be added to each audio sample for correcting or masking errors.

A relatively simple digital memory circuit places two samples of audio signal number 1 in time sequence and follows this with two more samples from audio signal number 2. The total of 64 bits replaces the television signal during the breezeway immediately following the end-of-sync signal. The audio bits are grouped into 8-bit words and undergo the same RAC-NRZ code process as the digital television signal.

At the receiving terminal, the end-of-sync signal defines the start of the audio bits. Audio processing involves time demultiplexing the serial stream into two separate sound channels, correcting errors, timing the samples at a constant rate, and finally converting the digital into analog signals.

Errors

A PCM NTSC television circuit can make excellent pictures with an average of one error in 10^7 bits (BER = 10^{-7}). The visibility of an error depends upon the significance of the bit in question. When the most significant bit (MSB) is wrong, it will cause a noticeable dark or bright spot. A least significant bit (LSB) in error will hardly be seen in the picture. In the interest of simplicity, error detection and correction techniques are not employed in the digital laser link. Operating ranges are such that the link is not power limited and threshold is exceeded by a safe margin.

Circuit Implementation

A parallel-to-serial converter, utilizing the RAC technique, and a complementary serial-to-parallel converter were designed and built. The block diagram of Fig. 15 shows the basic serializer.

The 8-bit, $3F_{sc}$ PCM television signal is alternately fed into two parallel-in-serial-out shift registers. One register is shifted out serially at $24F_{sc}$ rate while the other is being loaded with the current video codeword. At the next clock pulse, the role of the shift registers is reversed so that a continuous $24F_{sc}$ bit stream is obtained. Reverse alternate codewords are automatically provided by the inverter in the output of one of the shift registers.

A video sync detector extracts sync from the input digital bit system. It generates the start-of-sync and end-of-sync signals and inserts them into the output serial bit stream. It is essential for proper decoding of the serial stream at the receiver that the video sync region contain the correct word synchronization information. Correct sync tip encoding is automatically obtained if the original analog video signal is sync-tip clamped such that the digital bit stream from the A-to-D converter consists of all zero bits during sync tip. Then, in the serializing process, implementation of RAC generates a pure $\frac{3}{2}F_{sc}$ square wave during sync tip. The rising and falling edges of this square wave give accurate codeword synchronization as well as the necessary phase information to de-RAC the signal at the receiver. To guarantee correct sync tip encoding, the serializer detects sync tip and forces the digital bit stream out of the serializer to be a pure $\frac{3}{2}F_{sc}$ square wave during the sync interval.

In order to utilize the sync tip information at the receiver, it is still necessary to identify the H sync in the serial stream being received. This is done with a start-of-sync flag consisting of a three-codeword long (280 ns) all "0" serial stream at the beginning of sync. The serial digital waveform without and with the start-of-sync flag is shown in Fig. 16. This long all "0" digital stream is unique, and it can easily be detected at the receiver.

The start-of-sync flag generates a small dc component imbalance. It is compensated by a three-codeword long all "1" digital stream generated at the end of sync. This end-of-sync flag is a unique code and can be easily detected at the receiver to indicate the start of the PCM encoded audio inserted in the breezeway.

The Deserializer

The RAC serial bit stream must be converted back to a non-RAC 8-bit parallel codewords digital stream at the receiver. A deserializer, shown in Fig. 17, is used for this purpose. The serial bit stream is reshaped in the input receiver and is fed to what could be characterized as a tapped delay line. The delay is provided by a series of digital gates. Adjacent taps are separated by a delay time equal to the period of one bit in the digital serial stream. The start-of-sync detector generates an output when its input is all "0." Thus, at the start of sync, the long string of all "0" bits will result in a wide pulse out of the start-of-sync detector. Similarly, at the end of sync, the long string of all "1" bits will result in a wide pulse out of the end-of-sync detector.

The start-of-sync flag opens a sync gate that, in turn, is closed by the end-of-sync flag. A $3F_{sc}$ local oscillator is phase- and frequency-locked to the $\frac{3}{2}F_{sc}$ burst available during the gated sync tip interval. A sync confirmation detector continuously monitors whether the serial bit stream within the sync gate truly represents video sync tip. This is done by checking for the presence of the $\frac{3}{2}F_{sc}$ square wave. If sync confirmation is lost, the sync gate is turned off within a few hundred nanoseconds. This is done to prevent disturbances in the regenerated clock that would be caused by using a signal other than sync tip burst for frequency and phase lock.

The local oscillator provides accurate word synchronization to de-RAC the received signal. It is also used to simultaneously recover eight serial bits representing one PCM video codeword. The eight bits available at the taps of the delay line are simultaneously latched into an 8-bit register.

A more sophisticated system would regenerate the $24F_{sc}$ clock from the serial bit stream and detect one bit at a time. Although such a system may provide slightly better noise immunity, the simultaneous 8-bit detection scheme used in the link is quite reliable and much simpler.

The end-of-sync flag also triggers a sound gate which is 8 clock pulses wide (745 ns). Audio information that had been inserted into the serial bit stream in the breezeway can then be recovered.

The complete block diagram of the digital encoder-decoder used in the digital laser television link is shown in Figs. 18 and 19.

The digital circuits perform very satisfactorily. Noisy input signals that produce bit error rates of 10^{-2} can still be synchronized and produce a recognizable color picture albeit a very noisy one.

ENVIRONMENTAL SAFETY

The Radiation Control for Health and Safety Act (Public Law 90-602, 1968) gives the HEW Department the authority to regulate lasers where public exposure is possible. The Bureau of Radiological Health is the cognizant agency. Thus, what the FCC giveth, the HEW taketh away.

It is required that the manufacturer of the laser system submit an Initial Report to the Director, Bureau of Radiological Health, at least 90 days prior to the introduction of such a product.[6] Also, annual reports may be required, except that an exemption may be requested for a developmental prototype model. The Initial Report requires that measurements be made to verify the request classification.[6,7,8] Three classes apply to laser systems such as our TV link, and their emission limits are specified in terms of power output, power density, wavelength, and time of exposure:

Class I, the power output of which is considered safe for prolonged viewing and is exempt from control measures.
Class II involves devices that emit visible light and does not apply to the infrared laser.
Class III is more hazardous and requires protective measures as well as warning signs.

The Bureau of Radiological Health limits Class I laser systems to a maximum radiant power of 67 μW when the public is exposed for a duration greater than 8 hours. (See Reference 9, p. 36, table 5C for 820 nm and an exposure of 10^4 seconds.)[9] What is really meant is that the specified power may exist across an aperture of 7 mm in diameter, which is the size of the human eye's pupil.

The RCA 30131 injection laser by itself falls into Class III because intrabeam viewing can damage the eye. However, the television link system is

Class I because means are used to limit the amount of power that can enter the pupil of the eye. Although the injection laser emits 6 mW at 820 nm, a limiting aperture of 12° cone half angle in the transmitting antenna reduces the power to 20%, or approximately 1.4 mW, as shown by the curve in Fig. 20. This power leaves the antenna in a collimated beam about 10 cm in diameter. The waist (first crossover) of the beam occurs 100 cm downbeam. Maximum power density at the waist is 56 μW/cm^2, as measured by a calibrated Tektronix J16 photometer. This equates to 22 μW across the 0.39 cm^2 pupil area of the eye. The BRH limit for Class I devices operating at 820 nm is 66.7 μW through the pupil. As a result, the laser link is non-hazardous for viewing over an extended period (defined as $>10^4$ seconds).

There must be means to prevent the laser power from being accidentally increased beyond the maximum specified amount. Also, interlocks should be provided to ensure that the laser is de-energized when the protective housing of the transmitter is opened.

OPERATION

Aiming an optical link is relatively easy because the terminals, by necessity, are within sight of each other. The transmitter and receiver each have a rifle-type sight consisting of a 7 power telescope and adjustable crosshairs. We found it useful to attach high-intensity flashing lights to the terminals as aiming targets, especially when operating at night.

Good sturdy tripods are essential to support the terminals of the links. Azimuth and elevation are best controlled by geared, two-axis positioning heads. Pan heads used for cameras are not as effective as geared heads for aiming an optical link.

Measuring the position and size of the light beam can be accomplished by projecting the beam on a large sheet of white paper and front viewing it through a television system employing a silicon-target vidicon camera, which has excellent response at 820 nm.[10] The picture on the kinescope screen will show the image of the beam very clearly. Another way to view the beam is by means of a viewer that converts infrared images into visible images.[11]

The digital laser link has been field tested with good results. Picture and sound qualities are excellent within the one kilometer range. Improved antennas are being developed to increase the versatility of the link.

REFERENCES

1. Wik. Pratt, Laser Communications Systems, John Wiley & Sons, 1969, p. 128.
2. G. R. Elion et al., Fiber Optics in Communications Systems, Marcel Dekker Inc., 1978, p. 124.
3. F. Remley, "Reports of the Engineering and Standardization Committee Activities, Committee on New Technology," SMPTE J., 87: 331, May 1978.
4. A. A. Goldberg, "PCM Encoded NTSC Color Television Subjective Tests," J. SMPTE, 82: 649-654, Aug. 1973.
5. A. A. Goldberg, "PCM NTSC Television Characteristics," SMPTE J., 85: 141-145, Mar. 1976.
6. Federal Register, 40: No. 1218, Part II.

7. "Guide for Submission of Information on Lasers and Products Containing Lasers Pursuant to 21 CFR 1002.10 and 1002.12," July 1976, Bureau of Radiological Health, Rockville, Md.

8. "Quality Control Practices for Compliance with Federal Laser Product," HEW Publ. (FDA) 76-8036, Mar. 1976.

9. "Tabulated Values of Accessible Emission Limits for Laser Products," HEW Publ. 76-8029, Mar. 1976.

10. R. G. Neuhauser, "The Silicon-Target Vidicon," SMPTE J., 86: 408-414, June 1977.

11. Infrared Miniviewer, Model 7210, Electrophysics Corp., 48 Spruce St., Nutley, N.J. 07110.

Fig. 1. Digital TV laser link receiver (left) and transmitter.

TRANSMITTER

RECEIVER

Fig. 2. Block diagram of the optical television link.

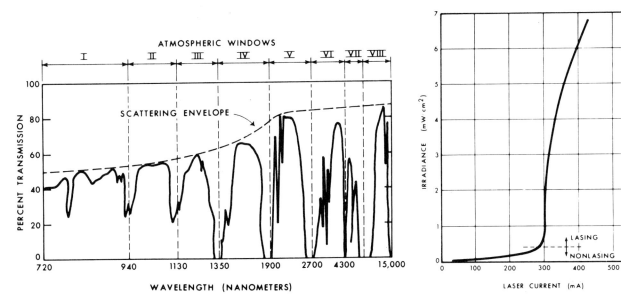

Fig. 3. Measurements of atmospheric transmissivity as a function of wavelengths.

Fig. 4. Irradiance vs. current of injection laser.

Table I. Comparison of detector types.

Basic Detector Type	Sensing Diameter Area(mm^2)	Sensitiv. At 1 MHz (dBm)	Responsiv. At Peak λ_o (A/W)	Bias Voltage (V)	Dynamic Range (dB)	Maximum Data Rate (Mbps)	Lifetime Range (hours)	Rise Time (ns)	Peak λ_o Response (nm)
PIN	0.3-3	-58	0.4-0.7	10-100	60	1-2 GHz	10^4-5×10^5	1-5	870
APD	0.8-8	-70	10-70	250-350	20	90-150 MHz	10^4-3×10^5	2-5	880

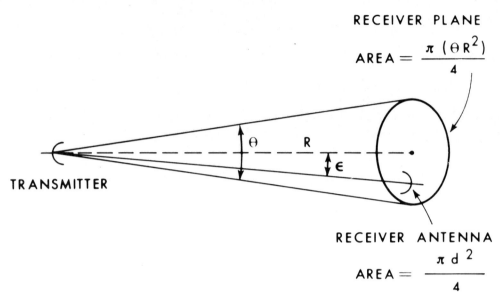

Fig. 5. The basic transmission-reception geometry.

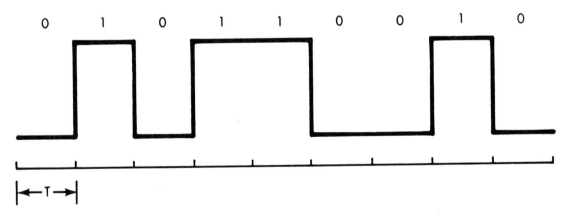

Fig. 6. A unipolar NRZ.

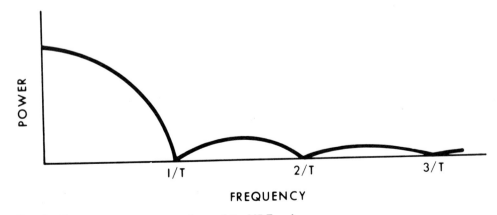

Fig. 7. The power spectrum envelope of the NRZ code.

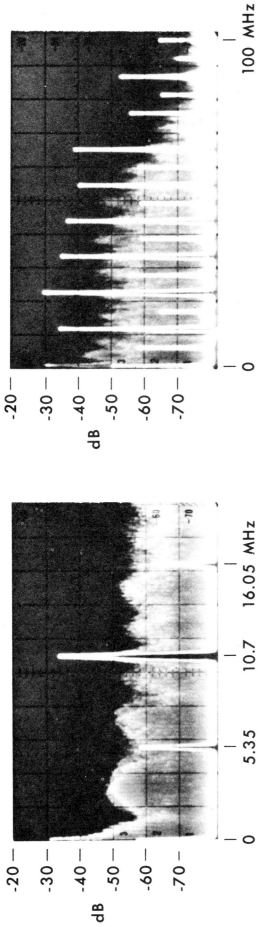

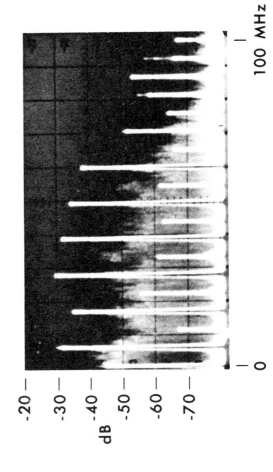

Fig. 8. The narrow spectrum of an NRZ PCM TV composite signal.

Fig. 9. The wide spectrum of an NRZ PCM TV composite signal.

Fig. 10. The narrow spectrum of an RAC-NRZ PCM TV signal.

Fig. 11. The wide spectrum of an RAC-NRZ PCM TV signal.

27

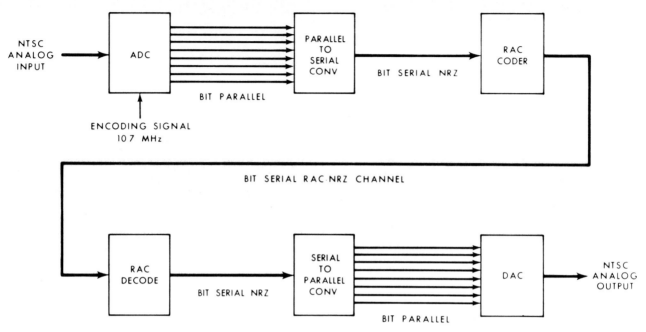

Fig. 12. Block diagram of a basic RAC-NRZ transmission system.

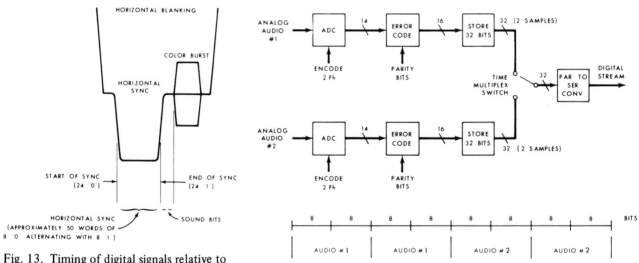

Fig. 13. Timing of digital signals relative to analog TV waveform.

Fig. 14. Audio digital coder.

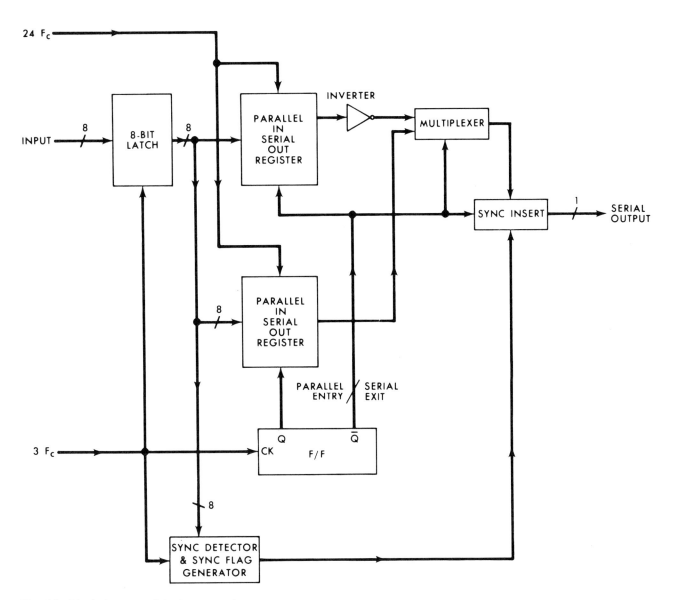

Fig. 15. Block diagram of the basic serializer.

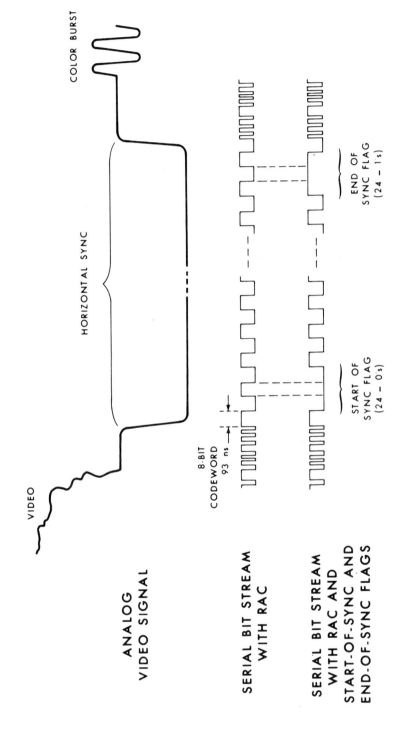

Fig. 16. Code format during horizontal sync.

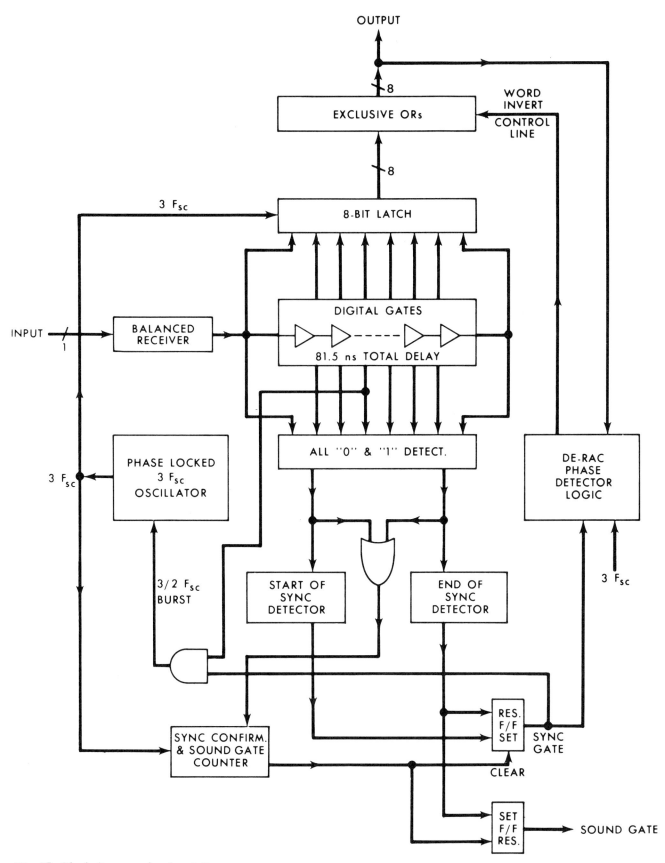

Fig. 17. Block diagram of a deserializer.

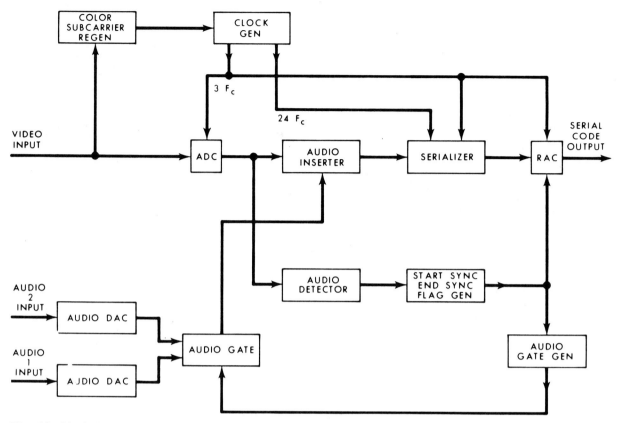

Fig. 18. Block diagram of encoder for digital video link.

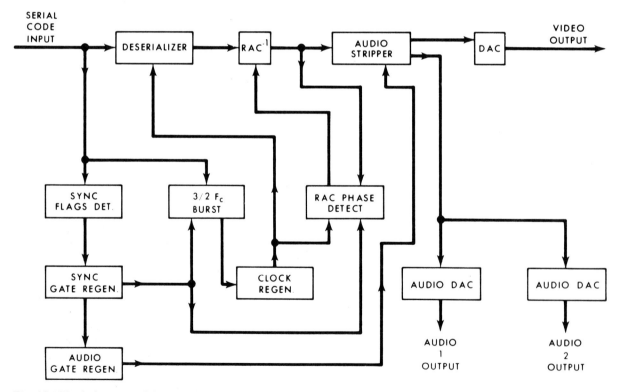

Fig. 19. Block diagram of decoder for digital video link.

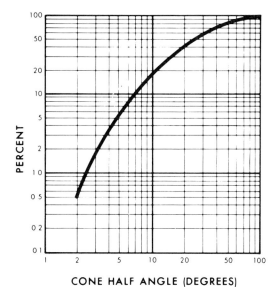

CONE HALF ANGLE (DEGREES)

Fig. 20. Percentage of total radiant flux within a
given cone.

Abraham Albert Goldberg is Associate Director, Television Research, at the CBS Technology Center in Stamford, Conn. He has been developing color television systems for 34 years, starting with the field sequential system and extending to digital television today. He holds 26 patents in these fields.

Mr. Goldberg serves on the following committees: U.S. delegate of CMTT to set standards for the international transmission of television signals, the European Broadcasting Union Working Party C1, a member of the SMPTE Television Technology Committee, and Chairman of the Digital Technology Subcommittee of the IEEE Broadcasting Group.

He is a senior member of the IEEE, a fellow of the SMPTE, and a registered professional engineer.

Stefan Juchnowycz is a Senior Project Engineer with the CBS Technology Center in Stamford, Connecticut. He was born in 1924 and received his M.Sc. in Physics from the University of Connecticut in 1972.

From 1956 to 1957, he was Process Engineer in the Semiconductor Division, Mullard Corp., in London, England. From 1957 to 1963, he was Research Physicist with International Philips in Toronto, Canada. He joined CBS Laboratories in Stamford, Conn. in 1963 as Project Engineer in the Electron Physics Department. He was Group Leader on projects affiliated with the "Lunar Orbiter Program" and the first "Mariner" flight to Mars. His present activities are in microwaves, electromagnetic propagation, antennas and lasers and their application to ENG.

John Rossi has been active since 1968 in the design and development of TV circuits in the Special TV Projects Branch at CBS Laboratories, now CBS Technology Center. In 1972, he joined the digital television study program which, under the sponsorship of CBS Inc. and the CBS Television Network, has been involved in a long-range development of digital techniques in television. This includes digital color decoding and image enhancement, adaptive comb filtering, sub-Nyquist encoding of NTSC color TV signals, digital-to-digital conversion, noise reduction, and special effects generation. Presently, he is a Senior Project Engineer in the Advanced Television Technology Department of the CBS Technology Center.

A Monolithic Video A/D Converter

Willard K. Bucklen
TRW LSI Products
Redondo Beach, California

For several years, digital processing functions have been finding their way into the television studio. The first large-scale application was in time base correction of video tape recorder outputs, permitting the use of smaller, lower cost recorders in broadcast applications. Since the introduction of the digital TBC in 1973, there have been fascinating new digital developments: special effects generation, noise reduction, video feed synchronization, standards conversion, and even transmission over digital networks and optical communication links.

Manufacturers and researchers are familiar with the many advantages of digital processing, but are equally aware of the high price of admission to the club. Changing a video bandwidth analog signal into a digital data stream is a difficult task. Converters have been developed, but they generally require over 100 components, careful periodic tuning, many watts of power, and a significant amount of space. In the same way that the advance of integrated circuit technology has cut the size and cost of a digital framestore memory by orders of magnitude, it has now reached the world of video data conversion with a single chip, 8-bit, 30 megasample per second (MSPS) analog-to-digital converter.

The Conversion Technique

There are many approaches to digitizing an analog waveform.[1] That new devices are being designed using a variety of these techniques is evidence that each offers advantages under certain circumstances. The three methods most often employed at conversion rates exceeding 3 MSPS are the successive parallel approach (also known as the feed-forward design), the stage-by-stage or Gray encoder, and the fully-parallel "flash" converter.

The flash encoder is a direct implementation of the analog-to-digital conversion function. An N-bit representation of an analog signal requires division of the allowable input range into 2^N discrete, predetermined levels and development of an N bit digital word indicating to which level the input signal is closest. This is generally accomplished by determining 2^N-1 thresholds or cutputs and determining between which pair of adjacent thresholds the input signal falls. The flash encoder provides a separate comparator circuit and reference for each threshold and the 2^N-1 digital outputs are combined to produce the desired N bit code. This technique is extremely fast and inherently monotonic, and a number of successful parallel converters have been built in discrete, hybrid, and monolithic form. However, the approach suffers from an exponential growth in complexity which has limited its practical application to 4 or 5 bit resolution.

Development of alternate conversion methods has been a successful effort to reduce the component count of the converter by performing encoding in stages, adjusting the analog input based on the results obtained in the present stage such that it can be accepted by a succeeding stage. Dramatic reductions in circuit complexity are realized, but at the expense of considerably more analog circuitry and a reduction in the conversion throughput rate (which can be restored through analog pipeline techniques, at the cost of more critical analog circuitry).

When the integration of an 8 bit 30 MSPS A/D was begun, a new set of rules had to be adopted: transistors are cheap and precision high speed analog circuits are expensive. A cost effective design for an integrated circuit is not necessarily that which has the fewest components, but rather one producing the most acceptable chips per silicon wafer. Minimizing the sensitivity of the circuit design to processing variations and reducing or eliminating post-processing trimming of the completed dice are critical to an economically viable product.

A sample of a time-varying signal contains information in the measured amplitude and in the time of sampling. Timing errors can be translated into amplitude errors by examining the worst-case condition of sampling a full-scale sine wave of maximum input frequency at zero crossing, where the slew rate is the highest. The error in percent of full scale, E, due to an error in timing, T, is

$$E = 2\pi\, ft \times 100\%$$

Timing errors are called aperture time and aperture uncertainty or jitter. With an input signal of 5 MHz, total aperture errors of only 64 picoseconds will result in a midscale level error of 1/2 least significant bit (LSB) at 8 bit resolution in addition to static linearity errors. As encoding techniques other than the flash method often require tens of nanoseconds for completion (aperture time), these conversion systems generally include a sample-and-hold circuit which has sufficiently small aperture effects and maintains a stable output during the encoding process.

Production of a video sample-and-hold circuit that does not excessively degrade the input signal is difficult and its inclusion adds another error source to the conversion system. A flash converter with strobed comparators is in effect a type of DIGITAL sample-and-hold, where the input level is maintained in the digital comparator outputs rather than as a voltage on a holding capacitor. The difficulty in implementing the strobed flash converter is in providing picosecond matching between 2^N-1 different comparators. The small geometries and close component matching of integrated circuitry make such a design practical. Physical dimensions are maintained with a tolerance of a few microinches and device parameters are matched to a fraction of a percent within a single chip. These characteristics, coupled with close parameter tracking over a wide temperature range, produce a device with performance characteristics unattainable in discrete assemblies.

The Chip

The TDC1007J organization is illustrated in Figure 1. The analog voltage input is applied simultaneously to all comparators, while a separate reference voltage is developed for each in the resistor string between V_{RT} and V_{RB} (Reference Top and Reference Bottom). V_{RM}, the Resistor Midpoint tap, is provided with a 15 K ohm series resistor R_T to allow a slight adjustment of the midscale point. This is necessary with a military version of the circuit operating at temperatures lower than -20°C to compensate an increase in comparator input bias currents as transistor Beta drops with temperature. The 255 comparator outputs are translated into a binary code within the three-stage encoder circuitry. The resulting 8 bits are applied to a set of exclusive-OR gates controlled by input pins NMINV (Not Most significant bit INVert) and NLINV (Not Least significant bits INVert). These signals permit true or inverted binary or two's complement output coding. The output latch holds the data until another conversion is complete.

The comparators are latched a short time (τ_{DELAY}) after the rising edge of the convert signal (Figure 2). The 255 to 8 encoding is performed at the falling edge, and the results are transferred to the output pins on the next rising edge, as the next analog sample is latched into the comparators. This "pipelining" permits the highest possible conversion throughput.

The circuit operates from +5 and -6 V supplies and dissipates 2 watts. The digital inputs and outputs are fully TTL compatible; though except for the I/O buffers, the circuitry is Current Mode Logic (CML) and Emitter Follower Logic (EFL) and operates from the -6 V supply alone. The nominal input range is 0 to -2 V (V_{RT} = 0 V and V_{RB} = -2 V), and a maximum of 30 mA is required through the reference resistor.

The simplified comparator schematic of Figure 3 illustrates the emitter follower buffering of the signal and reference inputs, level shifting diodes, and Gilbert gain cell. This differentially clocked circuit results in a comparator 3 dB bandwidth of 45 MHz and an acquisition time of 15 nsec.

The comparators generate an N-in-255 code, frequently referred to as a 'thermometer' code. It presents all ones below the threshold and all zeros above. The desired output code is the total number of ones generated, but such a 255 bit input adder circuit is not efficient from a layout standpoint and would require several pipelined stages. The alternate approach is to locate the unique point where the 1-to-0 transition occurs and mark this with a 1-in-255 signal which is readily encoded to 8 bits in an array of OR gates. The first encoding stage is actually performed by three-input AND gates which detect a 1-1-0 sequence to protect against random comparator misfirings within the range of zeros (Figure 4). These gate outputs are latched and held on the falling edge of the CONVERT signal, while the comparators are released to acquire the next sample.

As illustrated in Figure 5, OR encoding is performed in two stages: 1) Four 6 bit words are generated and latched on the CONVERT signal rising edge. One of these represents the 6 least significant bits of the eight bit output while the other three are zero. The OR function of these four words plus the two most significant bits indicating which word is nonzero appear at the output and are held when the CONVERT signal again falls.

Efficient organization of these various functions into a rectangular array is critical to circuit performance and cost. Figure 6 shows the general chip layout. The comparators and ANDing logic are arranged in four double columns of 64 circuits each. The center of each column contains distributed OR gates which terminate in latches feeding the final combining logic along the chip bottom. The I/O buffers are segregated to the side of the chip and are provided with separate ground pins to isolate the analog circuitry from the noisy TTL environment. The analog input signal enters the chip at five locations at the top and propagates down the outside of each column. The reference resistor of thin film aluminum (which is the standard ohmic interconnect) passes each comparator in turn, winding from the upper left to the upper right corner. The CONVERT signal enters the chip through a TTL/CML translator and is distributed to arrive at the head of all columns simultaneously. Here it is buffered and drives the columns. Though the propagation delay down the column is small (less than 1 nsec), this is still significant when effective comparator skew must not exceed a few psec. The analog input and CONVERT signal propagate in the same direction and their parasitics are carefully matched so the delay down the column is the same for both.

The result is a circuit employing 17,000 transistors and resistors on a chip measuring 261 x 264 mils (6.5 x 6.5 mm). The die is packaged in a 64 pin DIP with an integral heat sink, chosen to present a conservative thermal environment. With a θ_{JC} of 7.5° C/W and θ_{CA} of 10° C/W, the package can safely dissipate 5 watts, ensuring comfortable operation of the 2 watt TDC1007J over the 0°C to 70°C commercial ambient temperature range in still air.

The Technology

The TDC1007J is built with the triple diffused bipolar (3D) process, a refined version of a process used in early efforts to connect more than one active device on a single silicon chip. Its distinguishing characteristic is simplicity, requiring only 5 significant masking steps to produce transistors, resistors, diffused undercrossings, and a single level metal interconnect.

The 3D process has been used since the early 1960s in a variety of commercial and military applications, and currently supports a line of high speed digital multipliers and other signal processing functions. The technology was applied to the A/D converter design without modification. No post-processing trimming is employed; rather, precise control of photoresist tolerances and diffusion parameters produce devices meeting all analog and digital specification.

Support Circuitry

Two support circuits necessary for operation of the A/D converter are a voltage reference and an input buffer amplifier. These functions were not included on the IC as they would introduce several additional performance specifications which would in turn significantly impact the overall yield and cost of the circuit, while cost to the user and board area required for external devices are small. In many applications a major advantage is the flexibility allowed the system designer in making performance tradeoffs to enhance a particular characteristic.

The reference is readily generated from a standard fixed or adjustable reference IC buffered with an operational amplifier and emitter follower transistor to sink 30 mA from V_{RB} at -2 V. This voltage can be adjusted over the range of -1.9 to -2.1 V for full scale calibration or gain adjustment. The symmetrical comparator design provides wide reference bandwidth if dynamic operation is required. The V_{RT} reference voltage can be adjusted to calibrate the A/D converter zero point (because R_1 in Figure 1 is always greater than R, V_{RT} will be positive when the first threshold is 0 V); or it can be tied to analog ground and an offset applied to the input buffer amplifier. The latter approach is employed in the TDC1007PCB evaluation board, which offers the advantage of permitting a bipolar input range by providing a 1 V buffer offset range (Figure 7).

An input buffer is required because, though the input capacitance of the comparator circuit is only 1 pF, the total chip input load including other parasitics approaches 300 pF. As this value is largely a nonlinear junction capacitance and varies as a function of analog signal level and CONVERT signal state, it must be driven by an impedance of less than 10 ohms, and cannot be employed as a component of an input filter. The buffering requirement is similar to that of driving a 75 ohm cable. The LH0033 hybrid amplifier performs quite well in this application. If a closed loop design is desired, a combination of the LH0032 and LH0033 is satisfactory, or an emitter follower output stage can be employed (Figure 7).

Performance

The A/D circuit operates over a guaranteed range of 0 to 20 MSPS with a typical maximum conversion rate of 30 MSPS. Performance has been achieved under controlled conditions at rates greater than 50 MSPS. The chip will accept an input signal with frequency components of up to 7 MHz and convert accurately without a sample and hold circuit. For multiplexed data or higher input bandwidth signal applications using an external sample and hold, the converter will recover from a full-scale step input within 20 nsec.

Linearity is a measure of how accurately the converter thresholds are placed with respect to their theoretical positions. The TDC1007J has two components contributing to linearity errors: reference resistor nonuniformity and comparator offset voltages. The major portion of the nonlinearity detected is contributed by the comparators, producing a random code to code variation in threshold location. Other conversion techniques using fewer comparators, each at several places within the total range, often exhibit a repetitive error characteristic throughout the conversion range. The flash converter IC is produced without linearity trimming, yet generates parts which typically have no thresholds in excess of 0.2% of full scale (1/2 LSB) from the optimum positions.

Good differential phase and gain performance is critical to the acceptability of a product for broadcast television applications. Figures 8 and 9 show the characteristics of typical parts. The input signal is a 40 IRE modulated NTSC ramp. The converter is clocked at 14.3 MSPS, not locked to the subcarrier.[2] Differential phase is typically 0.5°, differential gain, 1.5%.

Signal-to-noise ratio measurements using the single tone test reveal an SNR of 46 dB with a 1.248 MHz full scale sinewave input. The system bandwidth is 10 MHz and the CODEC is clocked at 25 MSPS. A noise power ratio (NPR) test indicates the conversion system response to signals that are principally Gaussian in nature. The input signal to the CODEC is 4σ loaded white noise bandlimited to 10 MHz. Power in the reconstructed waveform is measured in a 1.248 MHz slot and then remeasured with the 1.248 MHz frequency notched from the input. The measured value is 36.5 dB, compared with a theoretical performance of 40.5 dB under these conditions.

Because of excellent thermal coupling and tracking of devices on the chip, these characteristics are extremely stable over a wide temperature range. The exception is linearity, which deviates from the specification at case temperatures below $-20°$C. As mentioned in the chip description, this can be compensated using the V_{RM} pin.

Circuit reliability is an important performance characteristic in any system. A well-designed silicon microcircuit has a failure rate which is difficult to measure by traditional methods such as a 1000-hour operation at maximum rating. A commonly used method of determining LSI failure rates is accelerated life testing. One can assume that the degradation of an IC to failure is a single thermally activated process. With this assumption, the Arrhenius rate equation can be used to extrapolate the shorter mean time before failure (MTBF) obtained at very high temperature to normal operating temperatures. The Arrhenius rate equation has the following form:

$$\frac{1}{t_f} = A \exp\left(-\frac{\Delta E}{kT}\right)$$

where

t_f = time for fraction f to fail
A = a constant
ΔE = the activation energy of the controlling process
k = Boltzmann's constant
T = absolute temperature

Considerable work has been published supporting the use of this relationship to determine IC device life.[3,4,5] It has been determined that an activation energy of 1.0 eV is commonly observed in accelerated life studies of bipolar silicon devices.

A recent test operated a population of 3D circuits at 320°C, and an MTBF of 100 hours was observed. This can be extrapolated to an MTBF with a case temperature of 125°C of 1.1×10^6 hours or 125 years (Figure 10). Reliability superior to other commercial technologies has likewise been demonstrated in the field over the fifteen year history of the triple diffused process.

Applications

The TDC1007J is clearly suitable for digitizing NTSC and PAL video signals to 8 bits for broadcast applications. It is also widely applicable to requirements in radar, ultrasound, and instrumentation. Capabilities can be extended by using it as a building block in higher performance systems.

A 9 bit flash converter requires 511 comparators, which can be provided by two TDC1007Js (Figure 11). With careful attention to the analog buffer and CONVERT strobe delays, this configuration can be implemented without a sample-and-hold circuit.

Higher resolutions can be developed with two TDC1007Js in feed-forward architectures. Figure 12 illustrates an implementation of a 14 bit conversion. Though normally the first converter would require a linearity accuracy of 14 bits, by providing one or two additional bits of total resolution between the two stages, digital error correction can be applied which will reduce the linearity requirement on the first stage to 8 bits +1, -2 LSB.[6] The D/A must provide 14 bit accuracy and 8 bit resolution. Fifteen bit resolution with 1 bit of overrange capacity would require 8 bits $\pm1/2$ LSB accuracy in the first stage. It is not intended here to minimize the analog problems in building a video speed 15 bit A/D converter. Resolving 1 millivolt in 32 volts at 5 MHz is difficult. Following the 14 bit example, two model TDC1014J 6 bit A/D converters (a small version of the TDC1007J) can be readily combined to product 10 or 11 bit data.

The Future

Advancing semiconductor technology presents opportunities for the extension of the monolithic flash converter into enhanced performance designs. The TDC1014J is a 6 bit version of the TDC1007J on a chip 1/4 the size which satisfies numerous requirements at lower cost and reduced power consumption. Increased resolution is of interest in many diverse applications, including television. Work is underway to reduce device geometries by a factor of three or four permitting the practical integration of 512 or more comparators. Smaller transistors also exhibit higher speed and lower parasitics, opening the way for converters operating at higher sampling rates and bandwidths.

The TDC1007J has met the television industry's long-standing requirement for a cost effective high performance video A/D converter. It is now contributing to the shrinking size and price of digital processing hardware. As the integrated circuit industry traditionally counters inflationary trends, continued price erosion is assured. With a video conversion chip, LSI technology has removed another hurdle in the digital television revolution.

Biblography

1. Bernard M. Gordon, "Linear Electronic Analog/Digital Conversion Architectures, Their Origins, Parameters, Limitations, and Applications," IEEE Transactions on Circuits and Systems, Vol. CAS-25, No. 7: 391-418, July 1978.

2. Michael O. Felix, "Differential Phase and Gain Measurements in Digitized Video Signals," J. SMPTE, 85:76-79, Feb. 1976.

3. D.S. Peck, "The Analysis of Data from Accelerated Stress Tests," IEEE 9th Annual Proc. Reliability Physics: 69-78, 1971.

4. C.H. Zierdt, "Some Circuit Considerations and Operating Precautions for Accelerated HTRB and Operating Testing of Semiconductor Devices," IEEE 9th Annual Proc. Reliability Physics: 79-83, 1971.

5. F.H. Reynolds, "Thermally Accelerated Aging of Semiconductor Components," Proc. of the IEEE, Vol. 62, No. 2: 1974.

6. R.E. Fletcher, "A Video Analogue to Digital Converter," IEEE Conference Publication No. 119: 1974.

Willard K. Bucklen received the B.S. and M.S. degrees in engineering as a departmental scholar from the University of California, Los Angeles in March 1975. He joined the Semiconductor Technology staff of the Microelectronics Center at TRW Systems Group, where he developed a configurable gate array for the implementation of logic in high reliability flight applications. Now with TRW LSI Products, he is responsible for the architecture and applications support of TRW's line of data conversion products.

Mr. Bucklen is a member of SMPTE, IEEE and Tau Beta Pi.

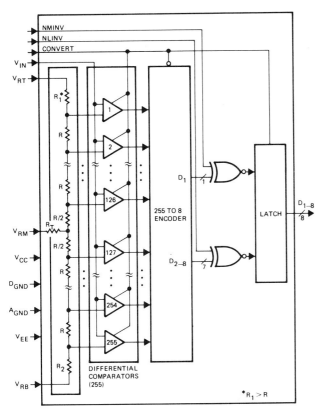

Fig. 1. TDC1007J block diagram.

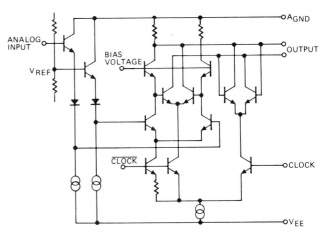

Fig. 3. Simplified comparator schematic.

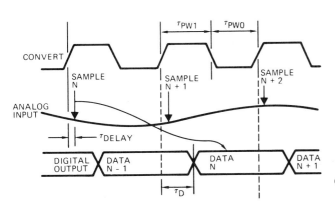

Fig. 2. Conversion timing.

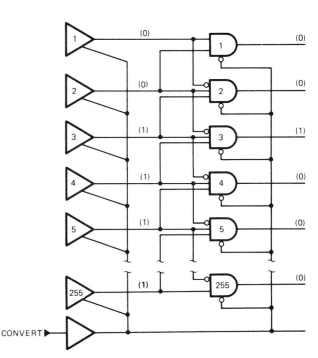

Fig. 4. AND encoding.

39

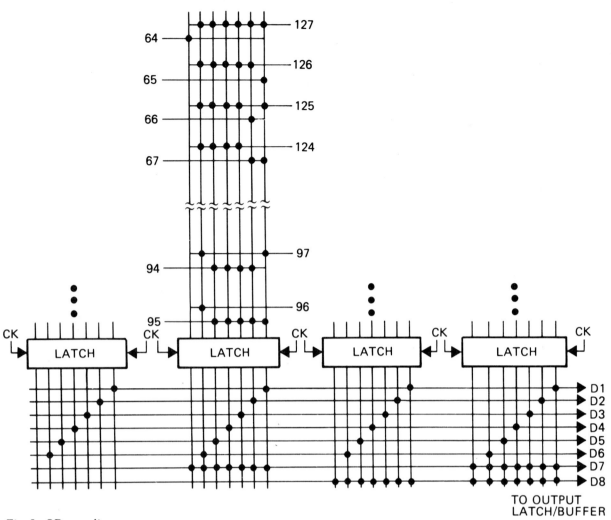

Fig. 5. OR encoding.

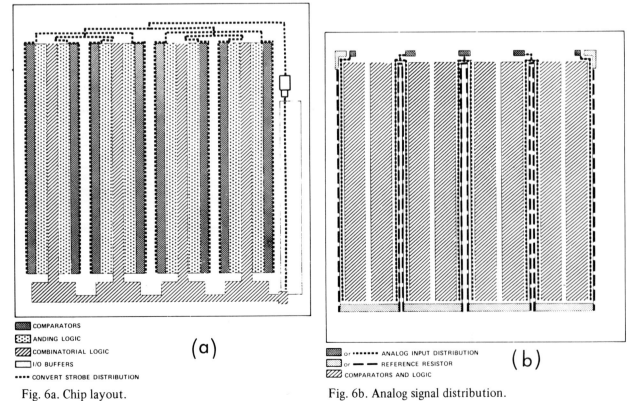

COMPARATORS
ANDING LOGIC
COMBINATORIAL LOGIC
I/O BUFFERS
CONVERT STROBE DISTRIBUTION

(a)

or .... ANALOG INPUT DISTRIBUTION
or — — REFERENCE RESISTOR
COMPARATORS AND LOGIC

(b)

Fig. 6a. Chip layout.

Fig. 6b. Analog signal distribution.

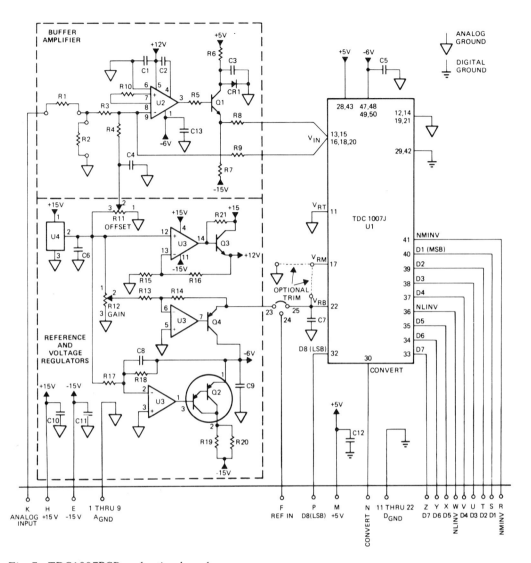

Fig. 7. TDC1007PCB evaluation board.

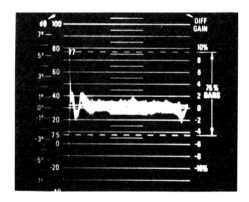

Fig. 8. Differential phase – 40 IRE modulated NTSC ramp – 14.3 MSPS unlocked.

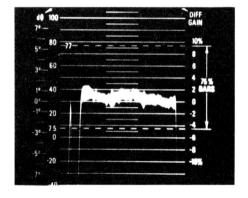

Fig. 9. Differential gain – 40 IRE modulated NTSC ramp – 14.3 MSPS unlocked.

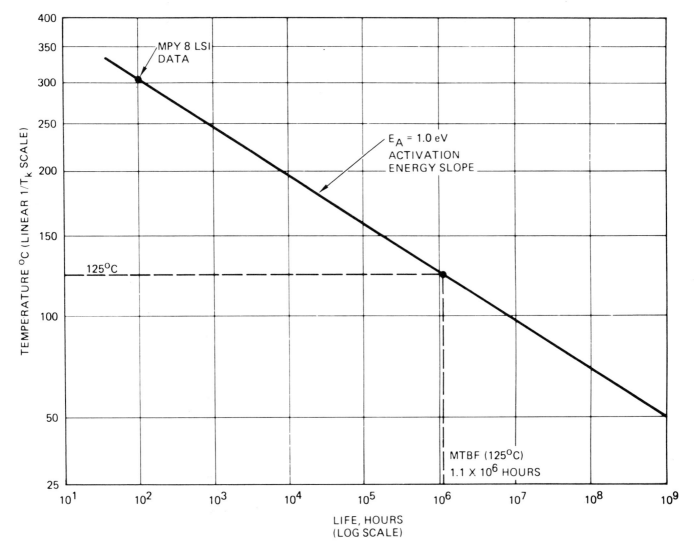

Fig. 10. Accelerated life test.

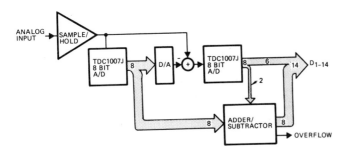

Fig. 11. 9-bit parallel A/D converter.

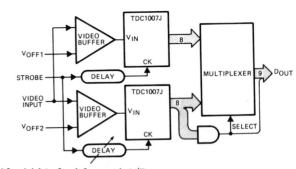

Fig. 12. 14-bit feed-forward A/D converter.

Digital Processing in the DPS-1

John D. Lowry and Richard Kupnicki
Digital Video Systems
Toronto, Ontario, Canada

INTRODUCTION

The DPS-1 is truly a DIGITAL Processing System designed
to perform a wide variety of processing and storage
operations on the television signal. These include
basic functions such as time base correction, frame
synchronization, and effects. Its design is based to
a great extent on the use of high speed computer technology rather than on the mixture of analog and digital
techniques found in a great many of the digital television systems in use today, which have evolved from
an analog television design philosophy.

MAINFRAME

A first and important step in the use of computer
techniques in video processing starts with the physical
hardware. This includes a mainframe, consisting of the
cabinet, a minimum of front panel controls, a card cage,
a modular power supply, a digital PC board format,
extensive use of large scale integrated circuits, a
wire wrapped back plane for simplicity in adding interconnections, and a standard video connector panel since
the system must interface with the analog television
world.

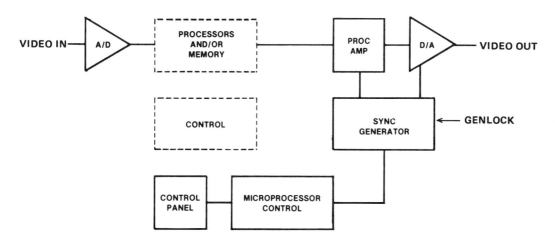

Fig. 1. DPS-1 basic mainframe block diagram.

The functions in the basic mainframe (see figure 1)
include the A to D Converter, a digital proc amp for
adding new blanking and burst, the D to A Converter,
a digital sync generator which can act independently
as a master generator or lock to house sync, and a
microprocessor for intelligent interface with human
beings.

Into this mainframe a broad variety of video processors
or memory configurations and their respective controls
can be added. In the DPS-1 all such processors
and controls are totally digital.

The basic standards employed include the use of four
times the color sub-carrier frequency for sampling,
and 8 bits per sample. The output sync generator and
video from the system conform to the RS-170A standard.

Standards for the digital interface of black boxes
will become increasingly important over the coming
years as more and more digital devices are used in
studio applications. Should digital data input and
output ports replace the analog interface, the mainframe
can be reduced to the mechanical frame, power supply
and wire wrapped card cage, complete with the circuitry
for digital input and output ports (see figure 2).
This will dramatically reduce the cost of the mainframe
which, in today's analog interface usage, represents
a major portion of the system cost.

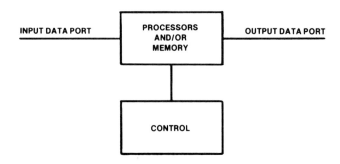

Fig. 2. **DPS-2 mainframe for interface with other digital systems.**

Processing or memory systems with digital I/O ports
can, therefore, be dramatically simpler, more reliable
and much less expensive. But we will obviously be faced
with the analog interface for some time to come.

ANALOG TO DIGITAL INTERFACE

In the DPS-1 the analog to digital interface consists
of one printed circuit board with an absolute minimum
of analog circuitry and associated adjustments.
The analog to digital converter is the TRW 64 pin
integrated circuit which has proven in production
quantities to be consistent and reliable, and when
properly interfaced with the video signal has

operating specifications of the highest caliber.
(Ref: SMPTE Paper - November 1, 1978 - Bucklen)

An all digital control system is made possible by the
use of a microprocessor. Functions such as video
gain must be accurately controlled prior to conversion
from analog to digital to make use of the full dynamic
range of the digital system.

In the DPS-1, a serial stream of data (see figure 3)
is distributed by the microprocessor to a register
on the A to D Converter board. 8 bits in parallel
are then converted by a precision D to A converter
into the control voltage for the video amplifier.

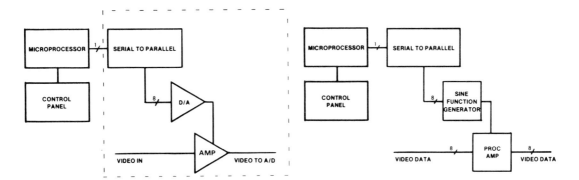

Fig. 3. Example of digital control over an
analog function, such as video gain.

Fig. 4. Example of digital control over a
digital function, such as hue control in
the burst generator.

Similar controls are used for black level and chroma
amplitude. An important advantage of this technique
is that the only analog connection to this circuit
board is video in. All other functions are digital.
This permits the free interchange of this or any
other circuit board from one DPS-1 to another with
no alignment for the individual system.

A similar digital control technique is used in the proc
amp (see figure 4) where the microprocessor sends a
command to a sine function look-up table, which in turn
inserts an appropriate word sequence into the data
stream, representing each analog amplitude required for
burst and blanking. The SMPTE Study Committee on
Digital Standards tentatively selected a set of digital
numbers that relate to IRE units (see figure 5).
The digital number 40 for example, represents blanking
level. To create blanking then, it is only necessary
to select the number 40 and insert it into the data
stream at the appropriate times.

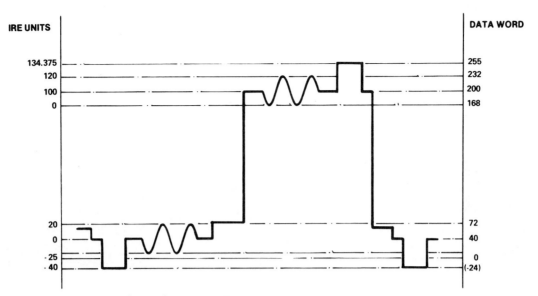

Fig. 5. Eight bit data scale in relation to IRE units.

BURST GENERATOR

The generation of burst is a little more elaborate in that we wish to create a sine wave. If four numbers of the appropriate magnitudes are inserted into the data stream in sequence, a single cycle of the appropriate analog amplitude can be generated at the system output (see figure 6). If this set of numbers is repeated eight times, the necessary eight cycles of burst are created.

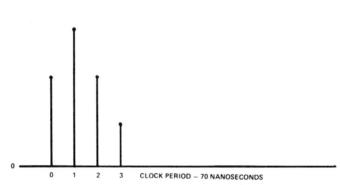

Fig. 6a. Magnitude of samples representing a single cycle of a sine wave.

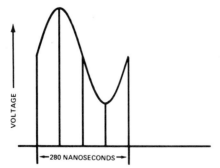

Fig. 6b. Sine wave after digital to analog conversion.

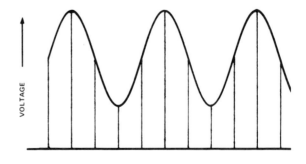

Fig. 6c. Repetition of the number sequence creating a continuous sine wave.

A further important consideration is the limitation
on the rate of change of the color sub-carrier
amplitude in the NTSC system. Burst envelope shaping
is introduced by a partial amplitude cycle inserted
immediately prior to and after the eight cycles of burst.

TEST GENERATOR

A similar technique is used for the generation of
digital test signals. Color bars, for example, start
on the left with the data number 200 representing
white, or 100 IRE units. The appropriate set of four
numbers to represent the precise phase angle and
amplitude for óne cycle of yellow is then selected.
This set of numbers is repeated 24 times to create the
yellow bar. Similarly, different phase angles with the
appropriate amplitudes are created for each of the
subsequent colors.

Using this technique, the DPS-1 provides a number of
test signals including color bars, modulated stairstep,
monitor alignment, flat field blue, color black,
linear ramp, and flat field 100% magenta which is an
ideal signal for evaluating the performance of a video
tape recorder.

Since these test signals are generated as a set of
numbers which are inserted into the video data stream,
and the D/A Converter has an output accuracy of $\pm$ 2
millivolts, it becomes a simple matter to calibrate
the digital to analog interface of the DPS-1. The
analog values for the numbers generated are readily
translated into IRE units for measurement on a
standard waveform monitor or vectorscope. It is
important to note that we are evaluating the digital
to analog interface at the OUTPUT ONLY. We are not
trying to calibrate the input and output at the same
time. The input could easily be too low and the
output compensating for it by being too high, or vice
versa (see figure 7a).

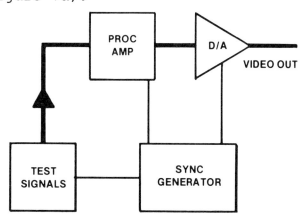

Fig. 7a. A basic digital test signal generator as used for calibration of the the
DPS-1 output analog interface.

INPUT CALIBRATION

After calibration of the output of the DPS-1, a switch
loops the analog output video into the analog input
section of the system. While the test signal is being
viewed on the monitor, it is also being processed by
the input amplifier, analog to digital converter, and
stored in the memory. The test signal generator is
then deselected and the information in the memory is
displayed at the output of the system (see figure 7b).

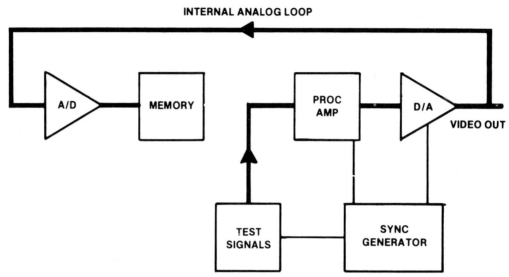

Fig. 7b. While the test signal is viewed on the monitor it is also reconverted
into digital data and stored in the memory.

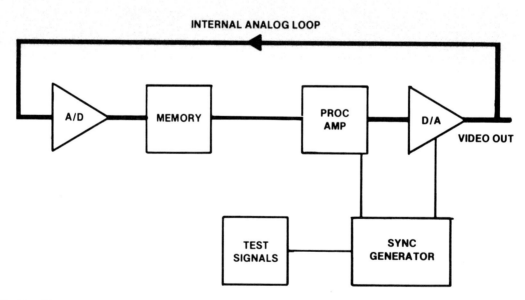

Fig. 7c. The memory is selected for display at the output of the system,
displaying a comparison of the test signal generator and the throughput
of the DPS-1.

This process is alternated between the test signal
generator and the memory to provide a display alternating
between the output and throughput of the DPS-1.

The input analog interface can then be calibrated
knowing that the output signal is already precisely
correct. The alternating display on the monitor provides
a reference which is often more critical to the human
eye than the same differences on a normal waveform
monitor.

For verification of proper system calibration during
normal operations, a touch of the unity button on
the front control panel in this split test mode, provides a display with no noticeable horizontal bands,
thus indicating the transparency and throughput status
of the system.

MICROPROCESSOR CONTROL

The microprocessor provides a precise and repeatable
control with functions such as hue rotating 1.4 degrees
each time the button is depressed. If the button is
held in one position for more than one-half a second,
hue will rotate at a rate specified by the microprocessor.
Each control range is divided into 256 steps, providing
very smooth adjustment.

An effective use of the microprocessor is to provide
interaction of gain and black level. When gain is
increased, black level is decreased proportionately,
and vice versa. The same holds true for the inter-
relationship of sub-carrier phase and hue. This
provides for a simple human interface.

Remote control and control from external sources, such
as computers or edit control systems, are greatly
facilitated using this completely digital control system.

The system can be turned off for days at a time without
losing the settings that were last implemented
through the use of a CMOS memory with its own battery
power supply. The unity control does not affect subcarrier phase or horizontal phase but is an ideal way
to return to a "one to one" system throughput, when a
new video tape is played.

SYNC GENERATOR

The final element of the mainframe is a truly digital
sync generator which employs a 14.3 MHz temperature
compensated high stability master oscillator. When
reference video is supplied, the system will lock to
station sync within one television frame.

The factor that makes this sync generator truly digital is that the DPS-1 does not employ a sync generator chip. All pulses are created by Programable Read Only Memories (PROM) which define timing to within ± 35 nanoseconds.

The DPS-1 sync generator uses the RS-170A standard. This standard is on the output of the DPS-1 regardless of the timing of the sync generator that it is locking to, provided that the sync generator that it is locking to does not have a drifting relationship between horizontal and burst.

All pulses such as blanking widths are programable to user specifications. This sync generator requires no alignment and does not drift.

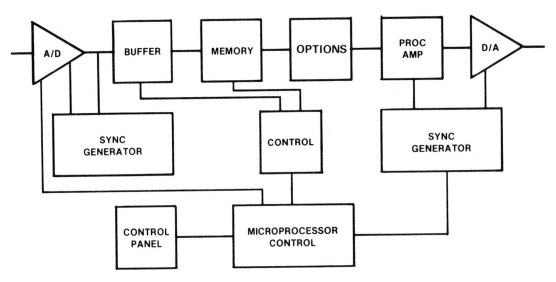

Fig. 8. The basic DPS-1 mainframe expanded to include time base correction.

TIME BASE CORRECTION

In time base correction an equally important sync generator is the one that must lock to the jittering input video (see figure 8). The objective is to provide a sampling clock which has a precise and continuous relationship to the color sub-carrier on the incoming video. To this end we determined that certain objectives had to be met including:

1. Precise line by line sampling phase error analysis.

2. Precise sampling frequency error analysis.

3. A format for the error information that lends itself to digital storage.

Again, a prime design criteria was that this sub-system must have no adjustments and it must not be capable of drift. We, therefore, chose a digital arithmetic approach.

BURST PHASE CORRECTION

The implementation of this arithmetic analysis is undertaken by summing like points in the digital stream during the centre four cycles of the color burst period (see figure 9). The summation of these points results in four numbers having an average of four times the amplitude and (in the analog sense) is the equivalent of a single cycle of a sine wave.

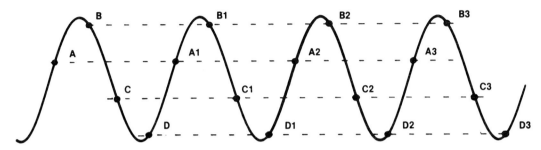

Fig. 9a. Sampling of the center four cycles of burst.

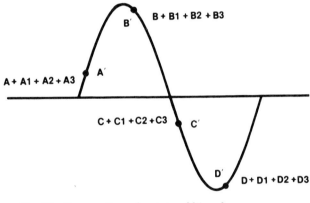

Fig. 9b. Summation of points of like phase.

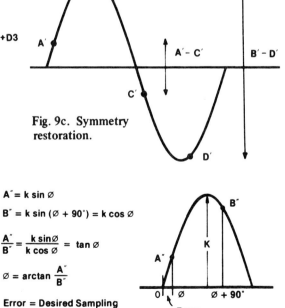

Fig. 9c. Symmetry restoration.

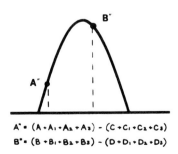

$A'' = (A + A_1 + A_2 + A_3) - (C + C_1 + C_2 + C_3)$
$B'' = (B + B_1 + B_2 + B_3) - (D + D_1 + D_2 + D_3)$

Fig. 9d. Two samples resulting from the summation and symmetry restoration of the center four cycles of burst.

$A'' = k \sin \emptyset$

$B'' = k \sin (\emptyset + 90°) = k \cos \emptyset$

$\dfrac{A''}{B''} = \dfrac{k \sin \emptyset}{k \cos \emptyset} = \tan \emptyset$

$\emptyset = \arctan \dfrac{A''}{B''}$

Error = Desired Sampling Phase - $\emptyset$

Fig. 9e. Derivation of sampling phase error.

This sinusoid should, of course, be symmetrical around its zero crossing. To ensure symmetry, C' is subtracted from A' and D' is subtracted from B'. This integrates the upper and lower halves of the sine curve.

The final result is two numbers A" and B" which represent the total integrated and symmetry restored information from burst. Since we are sampling at four times the color sub-carrier frequency, the samples are in quadrature, or 90 degrees apart. The arc tangent of the ratio of these two values will define the sampling position of burst, in numeric terms.

In the DPS-1 this technique provides a line by line sampling phase determination with an arithmetic accuracy to the nearest one-half nanosecond.

Any sampling phase angle error is corrected by adjusting the clock phase prior to the start of sampling of active video (see figure 10). Since any phase error detected is corrected immediately after the burst, the phase error detected at the next burst represents a measurement of the phase error that has accumulated over the period of one TV line. This, of course, is a measure of frequency. The phase error detected is both a measure of the sampling clock phase error for the current line and is a direct measure of the velocity error for the past line.

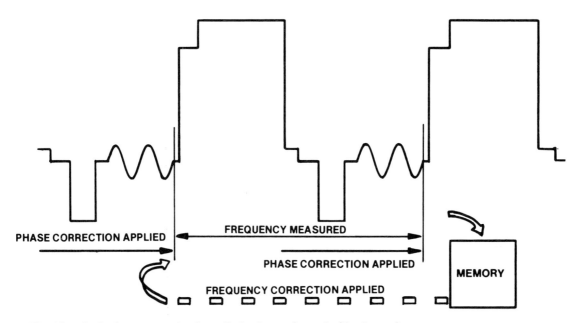

Fig. 10. Clock phase correction is applied prior to the end of horizontal blanking. Frequency or velocity error correction is applied starting at the beginning of the line in which the error was detected.

VELOCITY CORRECTION

The velocity error is defined as a signed 9 bit digital word which is then stored in a memory. When the video for that line is read out of the main memory, the appropriate frequency correction is applied starting at the beginning of the line, thereby implementing a look-ahead velocity corrector. The velocity error memory is matched to that of the main memory and can be applied to a 16 line, 32, 256 or 512 line system.

The results achieved with this arithmetic analysis of burst are a line by line phase correction and look-ahead velocity correction with one-half nanosecond arithmetic accuracy, that can be applied to any TBC window size. The technique is applicable to any VTR format, is totally digital, has no adjustments and cannot drift.

INPUT DATA BUFFER

In the DPS-1, Time Base Correction is accomplished primarily in a buffer memory immediately after the analog to digital converter. The objective is to transpose the video data from the input jittering clock to the stable output reference clock, for system simplification and efficiency of the main memory.

This is achieved through the use of four RAMs that are alternately written into with the jittering clock, and read out again with the reference clock. A single stable clock is then used throughout the rest of the DPS-1 signal path (see figure 11).

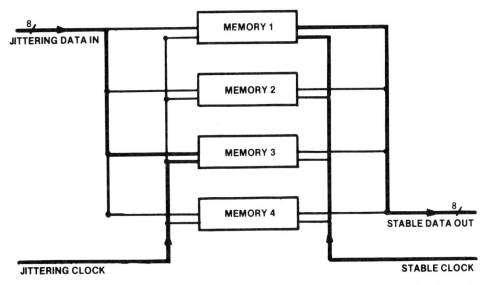

Fig. 11. Four RAMs are alternately written with the jittering right clock and read with the stable reference clock, providing stable data for the rest of the system.

MAIN MEMORY

Operating with the stable clock only, alternating between read and write cycles, the memory organization in the 32 line time base corrector has 768 picture elements per line, each having 8 bits for a total of 6,144 bits per line. With 32 TV lines, this comes to 196,608 bits which require precisely 192 1K RAMs.

We chose 768 as a basic operating number at four times sub-carrier based on the fact that it provides the full active line period plus 14 extra clock cycles to avoid the introduction of blanking problems. ' 768 is 3 times 256 which provides for excellent memory utilization in any digital memory structure.

By changing the 1K RAMs to 16K RAMs, a full frame store is realized. This frame store has 512 lines of actual memory which is more than sufficient to provide for the active picture, plus VITs and VIRs.

The DPS-1 Main Memory provides random access and identical organization for each memory size. The printed circuit board configuration is such that two of the 8 bits are on each of four identical PC boards. This provides for very simple memory failure diagnosis. A memory board with a fault can be plugged into the least significant bit position until the defective chip or the board is replaced.

FRAME STORE TBC/SYNCHRONIZER

The DPS-1 Frame Store/TBC Synchronizer has a system organization effectively identical to that of the 32 line time base corrector. The differences are an alternate set of memory cards, a microcomputer controller and the use of options such as the digital comb filter (see figure 12).

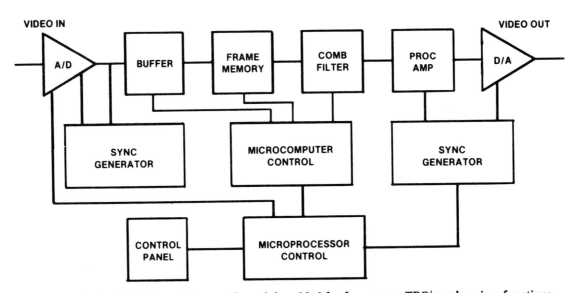

Fig. 12. The basic DPS-1 mainframe with modules added for frame store TBC/synchronizer functions.

This frame store can operate as a synchronizer or as a time base corrector with an infinite window. It can provide freeze field or freeze frame. It can be easily expanded for "optical effects" and through the use of a microcomputer control we have introduced a significant advance in frame store time base correction, namely, Frame Hysteresis.

FRAME HYSTERESIS

In frame store synchronizer applications, where the frequency deviation of the incoming video is continuous in one direction, the input to output delay of the frame store will vary from zero to one TV frame.

At the point where a one frame delay is reached, a frame will be deleted from the picture sequence thereby reducing the system throughput delay to zero. The delay immediately starts accumulating again until the instant where a one frame delay is reached and again a frame is deleted (see figure 13a).

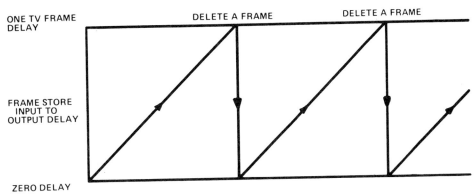

Fig. 13a. Delay behaviour of a frame synchronizer with input frequency deviation in one direction only, such as in the case of synchronization of two unlocked broadcast stable signals.

When the frequency deviation is continuous and absolutely smooth in one direction, the discontinuity of the occasional frame deleted, usually once every half hour or so, presents little or no problem in the continuity of a television program.

Frame store time base correctors have a rather different problem (see figure 13b). Once again, let us assume the case of a constant frequency deviation, but with time base jitter added. One example is the signal presented by any normal video tape recorder being fed back to a television station without time base correction at the source, or a playback without advanced sync feedback.

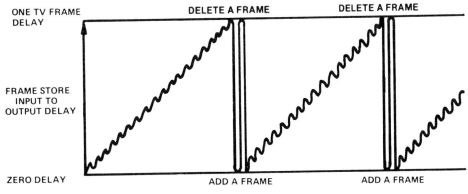

Fig. 13b. Delay behaviour of a frame store time base corrector with a slow average frequency deviation but with time base error, such as in the case of correcting video from an unlocked VTR.

As in the synchronizer, the input to output delay
will gradually accumulate to a delay of one TV frame,
when the system will instantly delete a frame
providing zero throughput delay. But now the jitter
on that signal moves it in the other direction for
a delay of less than zero.   The system will then
add a frame to compensate.

With a timing proportional to the jitter rate, the
system will alternately delete a frame and add a
frame until the average frequency deviation exceeds
the amplitude of the jitter, thereby moving the
input to output relationship beyond the indecision
period.

Once again, the input to output delay will gradually
increase to the point where the same delete a frame/
add a frame indecision period is repeated. This
obviously creates serious motion discontinuities,
particularly where the jitter component is high and
the average frequency deviation is low. The condition
is often seen on the air even with synchronizers in
the presence of noise on the signal.

The DPS-1 through the use of microcomputer control
has introduced FRAME HYSTERESIS. Again, the input
to output delay gradually increases to the point
where conventional systems will instantly delete a
frame, but the DPS-1 has a hysteresis period of 11
TV lines which must be crossed before that frame
is deleted (see figure 13c).

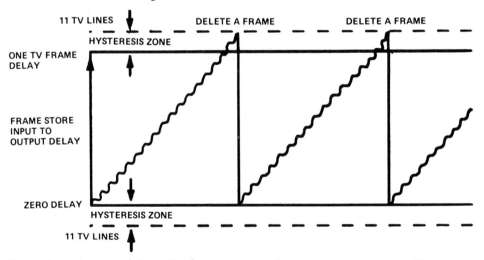

Fig. 13c. Delay behaviour of the DPS-1 frame store time base corrector correcting video
from an unlocked VTR through the use of hysteresis.

Similarly, once the frame is deleted the jitter
would have to be more than 11 TV lines in magnitude
for a frame to be added back into the sequence.
This notable advance in the use of frame store
memories is achieved by using an exceptionally high
speed microcomputer system and many months of software
development.

To achieve a similar hysteresis result with conventional hardware techniques would require a massive control system or a substantially increased memory capacity, either of which would dramatically increase the cost of the equipment. Using a microcomputer the hardware implementation is relatively simple with considerable PROM capacity remaining available for additional programs.

The DPS-1 microcomputer system also supplies the logic for field or frame freeze and chroma inversion. Periodically, during normal operation, it goes into self-test subroutines and displays any faults detected. Through the use of programable read only memories, (PROM) changes in the program are easily introduced into the system for higher levels of control sophistication and for future expansion including "optical effects".

FIELD STORE

The DPS-1 field store configuration reduces the main memory by one-half and is controlled by the same microcomputer with alternate program software. It provides a low cost synchronizer or a time base corrector with an infinite window. Once again, frame hysteresis is included. The field store can be expanded to frame store capability at any time in the field.

COMB FILTER

The next sub-system in the data stream of the DPS-1 is an all digital picture adaptive comb filter. You might ask why a comb filter?

Comb filters require the storage of at least one line of video and in their digital implementation a fair amount of hardware is essential, therefore, they are costly. Chroma decoding is common in the industry and uses very simple analog filters or heterodyning processors, even for systems requiring the use of a freeze frame.

In the NTSC system, any freeze frame or freeze field requires chroma phase inversion of every alternate frame to maintain the correct color phase sequence. This phase inversion at 15 cycles per second readily shows any differences between the chroma inverted picture and the original picture, as a low frequency flicker.

An excellent example of this flicker is in high quality pictures where luminance transitions are of sufficiently high frequency that they contain some frequency components that are in the same portion of the frequency spectrum as the color sub-carrier. When chroma is inverted, the luminance transition will have certain portions of its slope inverted also (see figure 14a). This is commonly known as chrominance luminance cross talk.

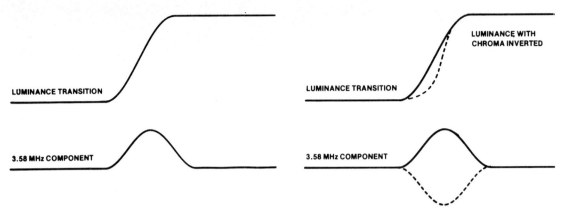

Fig. 14a. Luminance transitions in high quality pictures are often at frequencies higher than the color sub-carrier. The separated chroma signal will therefore, include luminance components.

Fig. 14b. Chroma inversion will invert the 3.58 MHz component from the luminance signal with a resulting distortion of that transition.

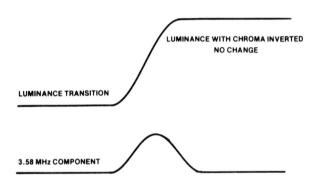

Fig. 14c. Picture adaptive comb filtering provides a near perfect luminance/chroma separation for full bandwidth, flicker free, freeze frames.

The resulting freeze frame picture will produce a flicker at 15 cycles per second in the fine detail areas of the picture. Any flicker at 15 Hertz is, of course, highly visible. One common solution is to roll off the frequency response of the signal to eliminate the fine detail in the picture.

The use of a **comb filter** can eliminate this problem and maintain full picture bandwidth.

Comb Filters make use of the chroma phase inversion on adjacent TV lines in the NTSC system (see figure 15).

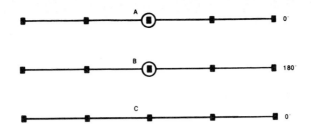

Fig. 15a. Comb filters utilize the line to line chroma phase inversion in the NTSC system. For example, $\frac{B-A}{2}$ = Chroma.

For example, in decoding for the point B, (B - A) ÷ 2 = a prediction of chroma indicated by the phase inversion in those two adjacent lines. This simple two line comb filter technique is often implemented in analog comb filters since no delay of the main video signal is required. It has the disadvantage of being a non-symmetrical filter and shifts the chroma information down in the picture.

A much better comb filter uses three adjacent lines with an algorithm that, in effect, averages points A and C. This filter, too, has its problems. Should you have a picture transition between points B and C, a notable error will be made in the decoding process resulting in vertical color smearing and incomplete decoding.

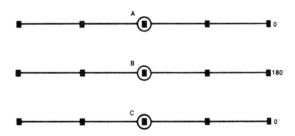

Fig. 15b. An improved comb filter averages the points A and C for symmetrical vertical filtering, for example, $B - \frac{A+C}{2}$ = Chroma.

PICTURE ADAPTIVE DIGITAL COMB FILTER

In the DPS-1, a picture adaptive technique is employed to change the algorithm when a vertical transition is encountered. Only the two lines that have similar picture content are used to predict chroma in the presence of a transition.

For example, when a transition occurs between B and C, the algorithm becomes (B - A) ÷ 2 = Chroma, or should you have a transition between points A and B, (B - C) ÷ 2 = Chroma (see figure 15c).

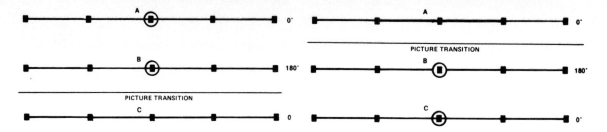

Fig. 15c. With adaptive filtering a picture transition between points B and C modifies the comb filter algorithm to $\frac{B-A}{2}$ = Chroma.

Fig. 15d. Similarly a picture transition between points A and B modifies the algorithm to $\frac{B-C}{2}$ = Chroma.

The result is a decoder or chroma inverter which provides freeze frames with full bandwidth, no detectable flicker in the picture and clean vertical transitions. The picture quality is such that high quality pictures can be chroma inverted without detection.

This totally eliminates any vertical or horizontal shifting of the picture regardless of the input to output color frame relationships for either synchronization or color frame editing. Color frame editing can be achieved with the DPS-1 with an accuracy to the nearest frame, rather than the nearest two frames.

The hardware implementation of this picture adaptive digital comb filter, is achieved with two circuit boards.

PROGRAMABLE READ ONLY MEMORIES

The design of the various digital processing subsystems in the DPS-1 has relied heavily on the use of Programable Read Only Memories (PROMs). These integrated circuits can be programed to provide specific output codes depending upon the input numbers selected. They are simply a form of high speed, high density, look-up tables.

A prime function of PROMs utilizes a simple counter, some kind of initializing pulse, and depending on the input count, each output of the PROM could give you pulses such as horizontal blanking, horizontal sync, burst flag, etc. The DPS-1 uses this technique to determine all blanking widths and other sync generator functions (see figure 16).

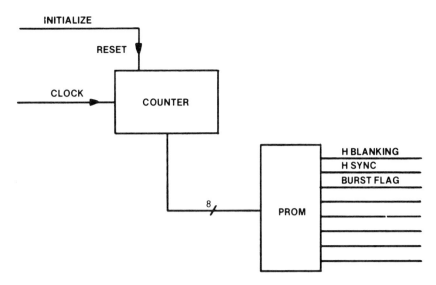

Fig. 16. Use of a Programable Read Only Memory (PROM) provides for precise conversion of a clock into a variety of reference timing signals.

A simple application of software techniques is that the PROM can be programed to reset the counter at any given number, thereby providing a great deal of flexibility for a change in the system at any time.

PATTERN RECOGNITION

Another application of Read Only Memories is in the examination of an incoming signal, to look for certain patterns or waveform shapes. For example, figure 17 represents a 6 bit input into the PROM which is latched at the output by each successive clock pulse. The 6 bit number on the input in this case is translated by this look-up table to tell us something about that point in time.

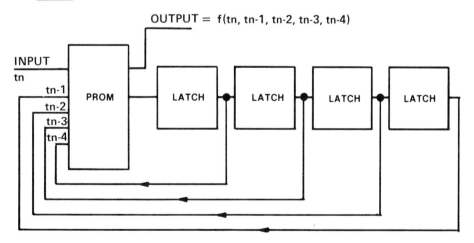

Fig. 17. Use of a PROM and storage for pattern recognition with respect to time.

This principle is easily expanded by feeding the output back into the input of the PROM and now with successive clock pulses we have at the output, information about the present and previous numbers. When another latch is added, we have information about three points in time and can start to examine a curve. This can be

expanded to any size, limited primarily to the number
of inputs in the Read Only Memory devices.
An important consideration in this technique is
that by examining the output at the centre of the
group of latches, it becomes practical to look back
and ahead. You can tell where you have been. You
can tell where you are going. This technique permits
the broad use of adaptive circuitry in digital
design.

Probably the most significant factor in designing
digital processing systems is that delay of the
prime signal is totally transparent. You can
examine where it has been, you can examine where
it is going, and then determine what to do with it.

Programable Read Only Memories then, are an extremely
useful device in digital circuit design. They can
be readily changed for any new standard or system
timing requirement. They can be supplied to customer
specification for special requirements.

Design improvements in the DPS-1 are often program
changes only, without PC board alteration. PROMs
use large scale integration today and are getting
progressively larger. They can't drift and they
cannot be incorrectly adjusted by an operator.

SUMMARY

The DPS-1 is a truly DIGITAL processor which presents
as close to a hands-off operating system as is
practical today for the playback of video tape. It
automatically adapts to input video parameters.
There are no normal operating controls inside and
most printed circuit boards have no adjustments
whatsoever. All modules in the system are totally
interchangeable with modules from similar systems.

Obsolescence which, of course, will come to any
electronic system in time will, in the DPS-1, be
at the printed circuit board, or PROM level rather
than at the system level. The mainframe will not
change.

The DPS-1 has exceptionally high quality video
throughput. An internal test signal generator
is used for instant system evaluation and alignment
and simple PC Board exchange can be used when
a fault is detected. The system has a broad range
of capabilities today and is designed for the
addition of further processing sub-systems in the
future.

John Lowry started his career in television at the CBC in Toronto in 1952. In 1961, he worked on the development of the first electronic editing system for videotape in cooperation with Ampex Corporation and Advertel Productions. Mr. Lowry spent six years in film production and was co-developer of the Wesscam stabilizer for helicopter photography. In 1971, he developed the Image Transform signal processing and videotape to film conversion system.

Mr. Lowry is now President of Digital Video Systems where he pioneered the use of the 4 times sub-carrier standard for digital video processing.

Mr. Lowry is a Fellow of the SMPTE and has six patents on video noise reduction, enhancement and film recording systems.

Richard Kupnicki has worked with television electronics for the past fifteen years, nine years of which have been in a professional broadcast environment. He received his BA Sc. degree in Electronics Engineering from the University of Waterloo, Waterloo, Ontario.

In 1974, he joined the Research and Development Department at Digital Video Laboratories, Inc., as a design engineer where he made numerous original contributions to the development of four times sub-carrier digital processing techniques. Currently, Mr. Kupnicki is Chief Design Engineer of Digital Video Systems.

The Near-Term Future for Digital Television —
A Panel Discussion from the 120th SMPTE Conference

NEW YORK CITY, 1 Nov. 1978

Edit. Note: During the Society's Technical Conference in New York, 29 October to 3 November 1978, a panel discussion was arranged to conclude the Digital Television Session on Wednesday morning, 1 November. The panel was comprised of authors of participating papers in that session and representatives of the SMPTE Study Group on Digital Television and of the Working Group on Digital Video Standards. Panelists and their affiliations are listed below.

Frederick M. Remley, Jr. (Chairman), University of Michigan;
L. Merle Thomas (Vice Chairman), Public Broadcasting Service;
Charles Ginsburg, Ampex Corp.;
Robert Hopkins, RCA Corp.;
Abraham Goldberg, CBS Technology Center;
Willard Bucklen, TRW LSI Products;
Yves Guinet, CCETT (a French TV research center);
John Lowry, Digital Video Systems.

Recognizing the probable impact of digital television equipment and processes on studio operations and program production, we herewith present an edited transcript — with questions and comments entertained from the floor — of that Digital Television panel discussion.

Mr. Remley: I would like to introduce first Charles Ginsburg, the Chairman of the SMPTE Study Group on Digital Television, and Robert Hopkins, the Chairman of the SMPTE Working Group on Digital Video Standards. They will explain something of SMPTE's present involvement in digital television and discuss the work of their respective groups. First let's hear from Charles Ginsburg.

Mr. Ginsburg: The purpose of the SMPTE Study Group on Digital Video Standards is to attempt to determine whether it makes sense eventually to digitize the entire studio operation — from camera through the output of the studio. We had our first meeting in February of 1975.

The people that have participated in the Study Group meetings are people who have achieved a good deal of eminence in picture coding and digital techniques. A number of reports have been written on the nine meetings held so far.

The Study Group recommended a couple of years ago that the SMPTE should establish a standards group and when this was done it became the Working Group on Digital Video Standards that Bob Hopkins has been chairing. They have reached some conclusions which he will tell you about.

Mr. Hopkins: The Working Group began having meetings almost two years ago. Our first meeting was at the NAB in Washington, D.C. and we have been meeting about once every 6 weeks on the average since that time. We made a report to the Society at the Conference that was held in Atlanta earlier in 1978 and that was then printed in the June 1978 issue of the *Journal*. That report discussed several basic points of agreement that this working group reached. We have recently begun writing a draft proposed recommended practice and we are hoping to be able to pull it all together into a document that will go to the parent committee, the Committee on New Technology which Fred Remley chairs, sometime in the first half of 1979.

Basically, we are looking at an interface standard. We are not talking about standards that apply within any one black box but rather standards that would apply in transmitting a signal from one box to another box. We have agreed thus far upon a four-times-subcarrier sampling rate. The reason that the sampling rate must be specified is that when two boxes, or multiple boxes, communicate with one another, parameters such as the frequency involved, the number of bits involved, etc., must be clearly spelled out. We have talked about an 8-bit system with parallel distribution of the bits between the various black boxes and a timing signal accompanying the data.

Mr. Remley: Before we take questions from the floor, are there any panelists who would like to offer questions or comments about the papers presented this morning on digital television?

Mr. Lowry: I'd like to ask Bill Bucklen a question. Large-scale integration is obviously very, very important in digital technology and it appears to be practical. If you could take a circuit such as a digital comb filter and put it on a chip a substantial cost saving could be realized even if the chip is relatively expensive. But then I don't know if the professional television industry is a large enough market to justify it. Could you consider putting sufficient memory and control on a chip to store an individual television line or a pair of lines? Is it practical to consider such things at this time?

Mr. Bucklen: Yes, that is a very practical consideration. As a semiconductor manufacturer, TRW is of course interested in return on investment. We are looking for a market large enough to justify a chip design and the production that is necessary to support it. We would be considered a specialty house in that we are more willing to address smaller volume production than the typical semiconductor company. The television industry at the present time *does* represent a large enough market to be interesting to a company such as ours for large-scale integrated circuitry. And we believe it can do nothing but grow.

Mr. Goldberg: I'd like to make a comment on some international implications of digital technology. The NTSC system was developed in the early 1950s and at the time we thought it was the cat's meow. Later on, the European countries came along with the PAL and SECAM systems, and various claims have been made of their superiority.

It's true: PAL and SECAM *do* have relative benefits in some areas. Now that digital television technology is evolving, however, engineers are more and more recognizing that the NTSC system has an elegant simplicity that lends itself very nicely to digital signal processing and coding. The PAL and SECAM equipment has to be a bit more complicated in order to do the same things that we can do easily in the NTSC format. That should make us all feel good.

Mr. Guinet: I must be the only European at this table. In answer to Mr. Goldberg's remarks, I think that the main reason that different systems were chosen was not primarily to respond to production requirements but rather to meet broadcasting distribution requirements — to get the picture to the public in the best condition.

I have myself always admired the NTSC Standard. It has very good architecture, certainly better than SECAM or PAL. This being the case, Mr. Goldberg's remarks apply only insofar as production is concerned and only for the present time. I think that digital technology is experiencing a permanent revolution, and as signal processing gets more and more elaborate it seems to me that components encoding becomes more and more advantageous relative to composite encoding, whatever the architecture of the composite video may be.

Mr. Lowry: In my opinion *Y-I-Q* or some kind of component manipulation is essential. Any special-effects system must use components to be really effective for manipulation of the television picture. I believe that one manufacturer of digital-effects equipment does not use components and that they will probably suffer due to a lack of smoothness of their picture manipulation. Certainly for any kind of sophisticated processing you must go to four-times-subcarrier with component coding whether you start out with coding as components or digitally separate into these components.

I believe there was a question asked from the floor just after my paper this morning. If you have it in written form, Fred, perhaps you could read it to us. I think it is relevant to the discussion at this time.

Mr. Remley: I think you're referring to the question: "In view of the rapid increase in digital technology, what steps are being taken to make this new equipment serviceable? Diagnostics? Signature analysis?"

Mr. Lowry: This is a very serious problem in the industry. Digital television equipment is reaching a level of sophistication where traditional servicing techniques don't work. It is extremely difficult to take a Tektronix 465 scope and a probe and find out what is going on on our microcomputer board. One way or another automatic testing of this type of equipment is essential. We have gone the route of putting in a software program which periodically keeps looking at various functions and I/O ports and says, "Yes it's doing its thing correctly." In our industry we must do this kind of thing more and more. It does have the disadvantage of requiring more hardware, but there are very few alternatives in the long term for servicing digital equipment in the field. You have to have a circuit board that tells you when it is sick.

If you want to carry this approach one stage further, alternate ICs can be switched in when a fault is detected, or with larger scale integration we may get to the point where within a given chip there will be an alternate circuit when one portion fails. One other consideration that was raised by the same gentleman was "Can you do it with a signature analysis approach?" Some companies, such as Biomation and Hewlett-Packard, have some very good digital analyzers, but this kind of equipment is not common at the user level in our industry and it certainly does not exist in the small production house where a lot of digital equipment is going to be used. Maybe the very large broadcast facility can afford the expert personnel and equipment, but the real growth in digital television, as I see it, will be in the production facility where technically it's truly a hands-off operation. You've got to produce a piece of equipment that the user can plug in and forget about the technicalities.

Ken Davies, Canadian Broadcasting Corp.: May I comment, on behalf of the users, that the things that we really look for in a digital system are interchangeability of components at a level where we can afford to stock them and dispose of them when defective. We are not really concerned about fixing them. We are really concerned about keeping the system online. We notice a trend in digital equipment to make it very complicated, and the acceptability of *this* equipment really depends more on low-cost, easy servicing by relatively unskilled people. I don't think that the television industry has reached the maturity displayed in the telephone and the computer industries in developing serviceable digital systems. Greater strides will have to be made before we can really start using this equipment in quantities large enough to achieve the promised benefits.

I also have a question: we feel that the acceptance of digital television really depends on the availability of direct digital recording of the television signal that we are going to generate. Would somebody on the panel be prepared to look at the near-term outlook for digital recording of the television signal?

Mr. Remley: I can't think of a better source to answer that than Charles Ginsburg.

Mr. Ginsburg: There is very little question that we are going to see digital videotape recording demonstrated more and more. It has already been demonstrated a few times, with a progressively improving system, by John Baldwin of the IBA. I would expect that soon, almost anytime, someone will present a digital videotape recorder and offer it for sale. I do not expect to see a *viable* digital VTR offered for sale for a long time. By viable I mean one that compares in price and in features with analog videotape-recording equipment available today. Some digital VTRs may be offered for restricted use, for example in post-production work, at a price that I suppose would be above that of presently available 1-in helical machines.

How extensive the use of such equipment will be is anybody's guess. My guess is that it will not be very extensive. The availability of a viable digital videotape recorder — able to do everything that available analog equipment can do today and competitive in price — is a number of years off, probably more than five. It depends upon many things, first of all on the basic technology of making a machine which can record and reproduce digitized television signals but also to a great extent on what happens with efforts to achieve standardization of sampling rates. If the recommendations of Bob Hopkins' group are adopted and a sampling frequency of four times the color subcarrier frequency becomes a standard (perhaps even if it becomes a recommended practice), then we would expect one of three things to happen to digital videotape recording.

In the first possibility, the digital videotape recorder would have to be able to operate at four times the color subcarrier frequency. This would create certain physical problems in getting the machine to be small enough, and possibly even cheap enough, to be competitive with available analog machines today. For the second possibility, a system might be devised which would make it possible, for example, to switch from three times subcarrier to four times subcarrier and back an unlimited number of times with "transparency" (in the sense that the system itself would cause no noticeable picture impairment) and at a cost that is bearable. If the cost of such a conversion system is added to the videotape recorder, then this would affect the economics and thus the marketability. In the third possibility, a digital VTR might be developed which would operate at a sampling frequency substantially below four times color subcarrier. Here, however, it would have the capability of interfacing repeatedly with other digital black boxes operating at four times subcarrier and do this interfacing in a transparent fashion. Again, the economics might be very difficult for the manufacturer. And any of these outcomes might be what we see about five years down the road. Is that a good clear look in the crystal ball?

Mr. Lowry: May I make just one observation in relation to that? You're making the supposition, of course, that you want to record all of the bits of all of the picture elements. I presume you have examined the various possibilities of differential pulse code modulation systems and in particular the potential of recording only the differences between television frames. I think there are some very attractive things that can be done in dealing with the frame-to-frame redundancy in television pictures. If you examine the frame-to-frame relationship of most pictures, there's really only 4 or 5% of it changing at any one time. The rest of the change is just noise. I would expect that somebody may turn up with a recorder using those techniques in the near future.

Frank Davidoff, CBS: I would like to ask a question that has been asked many times before, but I feel it is particularly timely, especially with this panel we have assembled here today. The question has to do with the introduction of digital technology into the TV studio and production house.

We all know that digital equipment became popular and got off the ground with black boxes such as time-base correctors, synchronizers, and special effects units. These, of course, all provided very special features that were not available with ordinary analog equipment. Today, we hear people talk about digital video recorders and, as we have just heard, there are differences of opinion about *when* they will come, although there is general unanimity that they *will* appear.

The question I would like to ask, and to as many members of the panel as would like to respond, is: "Where is the next application of digital technology going to be? Will it be in the introduction of additional black boxes into the studio, or will it be a complete digital studio with digital switching and digital distribution without any more black boxes?"

Mr. Remley: Thank you. Who would like to bite the bullet on that one?

Mr. Goldberg: I'm not going to bite the whole bullet, only a little piece of it. Frank Davidoff posed an intriguing, very comprehensive question, and it would take a long time to answer it. So I would like to make a philosophical remark about the application of digital equipment that I think will also bear on the comment made by Mr. Davies of the CBC.

At the present time, analog equipment is at a high state of perfection, but it does require a certain amount of labor to keep it adjusted correctly. This is because analog equipment has many controls on it and it drifts. Digital equipment − in principle, though maybe not yet in practice − is supposed to be built and hardwired or processed at the factory with, hopefully, no controls and very, very high reliability. Therefore, the objective of using digital circuits (other than in the special devices that Frank just alluded to) is to make possible highly reliable operation with a minimum of input labor, in other words to create systems that are really cost-effective. I think we should keep that in mind.

Mr. Hopkins: The digital equipment that we have seen so far has essentially

been performing functions that were either impossible or extremely difficult and expensive to do with analog equipment. I feel that equipment of this nature will continue to come along, steadily becoming more sophisticated and doing more things than ever before. Nevertheless I do feel that the critical point is in the availability of a digital recorder. I expect that when a successful digital VTR becomes available there will be a very fast switch to the all-digital facility.

Henry Zahn, Bosch-Fernseh: I would like to comment on the question by Frank Davidoff. The completely digital studio requires a digital *camera*, which is not on the horizon so far. However, this afternoon we will hear about a digital film scanner; digital switchers are already under development or on the market. And then there is the digital videotape recorder, which seems to be a viable item with the technology of today. Altogether this equipment is almost what is needed for a totally digital studio. In any case, it is sufficient to serve as a basic unit on the production and post-production level. Only one conversion is needed − the A/D conversion at the input of the system. All post-production work can be done on the digital level. And again, only one D/A conversion is needed at the output of the system to return to analog distribution.*

Gene Leonard, DaVinci Systems Group: I'd like to ask the panel whether there has been any consideration of adding enough additional bits so that we would be able to identify and manipulate individual pixels.

Mr. Remley: Bob (Hopkins), you're probably the one to respond to that.

Mr. Hopkins: The direction the working group has gone is to specify 8 bits per pixel, but recently we have discussed the question of whether we are thereby limiting ourselves too much in the future. Thus, we have decided that we should include in this interface two spare sets of wires that could, if desired, be used for a ninth and tenth bit system. In fact, we would specify what those connections would be, although our proposal would be for an 8-bit system.

Mr. Lowry: There is a point that

---

*Mr. Zahn incidentally called attention to the biennial Montreux Symposium scheduled for May 27 to June 1, 1979. As Topics Chairman of the session on Digital Recording Equipment (John Baldwin chaired the more scientific session on Digital Recording Technologies), he issued a call for papers from manufacturers of digital video recording equipment − to describe their concepts or actual systems.

Bob didn't touch on. The standard that we have been discussing in the committee deals with line numbering rather than just having a horizontal sync pulse. We are actually identifying what line we are on at any given moment. It doesn't directly identify the individual picture element, but it gets you very close to it.

Mr. Hopkins: I'd like to make a comment also on the question of the digital camera. I think there is an implication here that I would have to disagree with slightly. The comment was made that there will be a paper describing a digital telecine. My understanding is that there is an A to D converter used in that system, and I think we should be careful not to imply that this is an all-digital telecine or camera, in terms of the original pick-up.

Mr. Remley: There is one point that should be made about the papers we've heard this morning and the discussions that followed. I think Al Goldberg is the only one who has mentioned the audio signal, and I must say that that was done fairly briefly. I don't intend to open a discussion of digital audio, but I think there are probably opinions that need a bit of airing. First of all, in the discussions on digital processing, I'm sure I'm correct in saying that by the time you go through a number of processing systems, the delays certainly accumulate to the point where some consideration must be taken of the audio accompanying the video. In other words, we will have a plant that will be digital in terms of both aural and visual elements at some point, won't we?

Mr. Hopkins: With respect to the standard or proposed standard that we have talked about, we are not dealing with audio. However, in the timing signal that accompanies the video, we have made provisions for, in the future, incorporating data that would indicate the delay that the video had experienced in going through that box so that this type of signal could be used in some other box to delay the audio an equivalent amount.

Mr. Lowry: An observation, for what it's worth, on the frame synchronizer problem. Obviously if you have a number of synchronizers in the chain and somebody adds a special-effects system, you could be off a number of frames from the original lip sync. Anything over two frames difference is usually unacceptable, since some people can see a 1½-frame lip-sync error. Certainly two frames is bad, and today you can often get that many framestores in cascade and sometimes even 4 or 5. We should be doing something about it, but it takes more than just matching an audio delay with the video synchronizer. You cannot accumulate an audio delay and then drop out a thirtieth of a second as we do with pictures; you'll hear it. There are a lot of considerations that really need to be looked into. Digital audio synchronization will require at least fourteen-bit accuracy and hopefully a clock rate that has some direct relationship to the video sampling frequency. Certainly it is something that

we should be addressing ourselves to, but quite frankly I don't think that many video organizations are giving it the attention that they should.

Mr. Remley: I think the industry will begin addressing it effectively over the next few months. I assume that the semiconductor industry will be giving it some thought too. I think that everything we have heard today from the panelists and others indicates

pretty clearly that when there is a need expressed and there is a probable market, the technology is usually not far away.

If there are no further questions or statements, I think that this is a good point to conclude this morning's session. I appreciate, of course, the help of the panelists, and the audience has been most responsive and helpful as well. Thank you all very much.

The Expanding World of Digital Video Effects

Richard John Taylor
Quantel Limited
Newbury, Berkshire, England

INTRODUCTION

The accelerating pace of the development of digital techniques for
television has presented the Broadcaster with an interesting dilemma. On
the one hand he sees the power of the techniques to provide solutions to
engineering problems, extend existing capabilities and create new effects
and thus applies pressure to the industry to speed up development. On the
other hand, he sees that very pressure bringing with it the high probability of equipment purchased this year being obsolescent next year.

An ideal solution to his dilemma would be a system similar to the digital
computer that has become an entirely 'general purpose' piece of equipment
where the same unit can fulfil many different tasks merely by re-programing
the processor. Regrettably, digital video systems have, until recently,
been unable to enjoy this flexibility since often the equipment has had to
be in the form of very special purpose hardware optimized for a single
function.

The field in which the problem of 'instant obsolescence' is perhaps
greatest is that of video effects. However, a new generation of digital
effects equipment is now emerging that have a much higher degree of software orientation. Field experience is proving that such devices allow
users to be kept fully up to date with the latest development each year
by the expedient of merely purchasing new programs for existing machines
rather than buying complete replacement units.

It is the purpose of this paper to trace the history of just such an
equipment - the Quantel DPE 5000 Digital Production Effects system -
discussing the background to the design and showing how options and new
facilities have grown from the original form of the equipment.

BACKGROUND

Although the subject of this paper is a digital video effects unit
designed for the real-time manipulation of TV images, the story would not
be complete without reference to a device called 'INTELLECT', since the
background to all Quantel's picture manipulation equipment is deeply
rooted in this machine. Shown in Figure 1, INTELLECT is an equipment
devised by Micro Consultants Limited some four years ago primarily to
satisfy the specialist image processing market.

The purpose of INTELLECT is to allow the user total freedom and flexibility
to analyse, process or synthesise a picture entirely by software. In other
words, it is best described as a general purpose computer that is able to
'see'.

Figure 2 shows the basic block diagram. It is clear that the heart of the
device is a framestore. In common with all the Company's framestores the
memory is able to capture in real-time video information from a camera,

VTR or similar source and reproduce the information on a standard TV monitor, but the aspect of the machine that makes it unique is the computer port on the store since, simultaneously with information being received from a camera and displayed on the monitor, a powerful mini-computer is allowed truly random access to the store.

Thus, by taking information from the camera into the computer via the store, pictures can be analysed, or by asking the computer to 'write' into the store and then on to the display, pictures can be synthesised, but, most powerful of all, by using a combination of the two, pictures can be processed.

Since the computer has access at complete random to any pixel or group of pixels in the store, clearly the level of processing and manipulation achievable is purely limited by the ingenuity and imagination of the programmer.

INTELLECT is perhaps the only equipment that approaches the ideal goal of a 'general purpose' video processor for the broadcaster since, as has been explained, the flexibility of the machine allows virtually any conceivable form of manipulation or effect to be created. However, regrettably that very flexibility forces the processing functions to be slow, so that even when very powerful computers are employed still several tens of seconds are required to process a single frame.

Notwithstanding this speed limitation, this unique machine has found applications in a multitude of different fields ranging from medical electronics to space research, or from radar simulators to television cartoon drawings, but, not least, INTELLECT is to be found in the development laboratory as a tool to perfect image processing techniques for the broadcaster.

EXPERIMENTS LEADING TO THE DPE 5000

Clearly, if INTELLECT were a truly real-time machine it would be the ideal solution to the broadcasters' dilemma - infinitely flexible so that any effect or manipulation of the video would be possible by software alone. However, whilst this ultimate goal of an entirely general purpose real-time broadcast video processor still remains unattainable, an excellent compromise is possible in the field of digital video effects where only a small degree of flexibility needs to be lost to gain a very significant increase in speed.

Experiments were, therefore, carried out using INTELLECT to perfect fixed algorithms that would allow the basic pre-requisite of video effects devices, the modification of the size, shape and position of the TV picture, to be performed with a fidelity that rivalled film optical techniques.

It is interesting to note that some 30 different algorithms were investigated before the correct set were found. For each of those sets to have been tried in hardware would have taken many years - as it was, even the most complex took less than one minute per frame in the INTELLECT computer.

THE SYSTEM DEFINITION

Until recently the medium of celluloid has been able to keep the field of video special effects, involving changing the shape or position of an image, entirely to itself. However, the advent of digital video effects systems has now broken that monopoly, not only obviating the need to dub from video tape to film and thence from 'modified' film back to tape, but also allowing the 'optical' effect to be performed in real-time.

In the design of the DPE 5000 Digital Production Effects system three goals had to be satisfied if the 'electronic' equipment was to genuinely replace the film optical. First, the same effects achievable with opticals had to be capable of creation in real-time. Second, these effects had to be achieved with a fidelity highly competitive with the film medium, ensuring that Directors and Producers paid no penalty in quality when manipulating picture live on air and, last but not least, the equipment had to be capable of field upgrade as new effects became possible.

THE DPE 5000

The experiments in the theory of picture manipulation being completed, the hardware for the DPE 5000 was designed.

The hardware is shown in Figure 3 and can be seen to be highly compact, comprising three main elements; the main picture processor in $12\frac{1}{4}$ inches of rack space; a DEC LSI-11 mini-computer as system controller in $3\frac{1}{2}$ inches of rack space and an operator's control panel designed for desk mounting.

The basic effects that the initial equipment was to perform were those associated with the expansion of the live TV picture up to four times full size, and the variable compression to a pinpoint. Reframing the image and changing the aspect ratio were also included in the machines definition.

Figure 4 shows a very basic block diagram of the system. The proliferation of computers and micro processors is immediately noticeable. The decision to base the equipment around a distributed array of computers was made on two counts: firstly, a substantial increase in speed is obtained by allowing several processors to operate in parallel: secondly, it is possible to ensure that each section of the machine is self-contained with information being exchanged between sections being via high level commands. This latter concept has most significance when it comes to subsequent expansion of the system.

The machine can be regarded as being in three parts. The arithmetic unit and associated digital video signal processing, the master controlling computer and the control systems themselves.

The Arithmetic Unit

The heart of the machine is again a framestore but this time a special purpose arithmetic hardware unit is associated with the store in such a way that all the stored pixels relevant to the generation of one output pixel can be fed into the special hardware to perform the necessary algorithms. Of course a complex addressing system is also required to operate both the store and the arithmetic unit.

Now it is necessary, at chosen points in the frame, to set various parameters, calculate co-efficients and route information.

70

All these functions are achieved by means of a micro processor.

The micro processor is a Motorola 6800 working on a common bus feeding the entire backplane of the rack so that control parameters to co-efficients can be routed to the requisite cards.

The arithmetic unit, framestore, addressing system and 6800 computer all form one self-contained section of the equipment with an interface of simple digital video signals and high level commands.

The high level commands into the 6800 take the form of digital numbers specifying horizontal width, horizontal position, vertical height and vertical position.

At this point it is clear that, although the actual algorithms are implemented in fixed hardware, a high degree of flexibility is possible if the software in the 6800 is modified to change algorithms, address co-efficients and controls.

The Master Computer

The master computer for the system is a DEC LSI-11 mini-computer. A computer of this power was chosen to allow later flexibility as well as advanced control concepts to permit easy handling of the very wide dynamic range capable of the arithmetic unit.

The LSI-11 is responsible for all size and shape changes of the picture, as well as re-positioning the image, shaping of the pre-set moves from the control panel, conversion of analogue information from control joysticks, generation of compressed picture border within NTSC specification, and a host of other 'house-keeping' tasks.

All commands from the control panel are routed to the LSI-11 to be converted eventually to the basic commands understood by the 6800 in the arithmetic unit.

The power of this approach is apparent in the ease with which the equipment is controlled, the simplicity of updating the software of the machine and the successful subsequent expansion of the system.

An example of a complex task carried out by the LSI-11 is the shaping of a move from one preselected image position and size, programed on the control panel, to another. A simple linear move over a given time was found to look 'artificial' on the screen. As an alternative, the LSI-11 computes an over-damped simple harmonic motion speed profile that exactly matches the pan or tilt motion of a heavy pedestal camera moved by a camera man. The pleasing 'electronic' result is quite indistinguishable from the 'human' result.

The Controls

The DPE 5000 has three main modes of operation. It can be used as a stand alone device, integrated with a key generator for

auto key tracking or totally integrated with a production switcher.
This arrangement enables an operator to manipulate the picture from
the control panel, from the camera, from the switcher control arms
or from a combination of all three. Once again, it is the flexibility
of the software approach to the machine that largely permits this
freedom.

The Operator's Control Panel

The 'stand alone' operator's control panel contains the third
computer in the system - an Intel 8748 single chip micro
processor that is used simply to light lights, drive LED
displays and multiplex switch data.

The panel has been optimized to allow great freedom and yet
also satisfy the requirement of allowing simple 'first time
take' in a live situation.

The control panel is shown in Figure 5. It is felt that a
detailed description of the operation of the system is not
appropriate here, although it is worthwhile discussing the
most commonly used facility in the panel - the 'preselect'
buttons. This facility allows the status of the size and
position of an image, once set by the joysticks, to be
recorded in any of the preselect buttons by depressing the
chosen 'preselect' location together with the 'enter' button.

Subsequent depression of that chosen preselect button will
always ensure instant return to the previously programed
size and position of the picture. The transition time for
the picture to arrive at this new situation can also be
programed by setting the appropriate number of frames required
on the size rate and position rate LEDs with the toggle
switches provided. Whatever setting is present on these LEDs
when the enter button with chosen preselect location is
depressed will be memorized. Subsequent depression of the
chosen location will move the picture to the required size
and position with the SHM speed profile.

Auto Key

Auto key is the means by which the 5000 can be automatically
controlled from a foreground camera with a chroma key area
in view.

The method of control is to feed the DPE 5000 with the key
shape derived by a key generator from the foreground camera.
The 5000 then computes the size and shape of the key, automatically compressing the image to fit in the 'hole'.

Because the compression is then controlled by the key itself,
the foreground camera is free to pan, tilt and zoom whilst
the 5000 ensures that at all times the compressed video tracks
and fills the 'hole'.

It will be seen from Figure 4 that this measurement of the key
size and shape is achieved by the fourth computer in the

72

machine - in this case the 2900 bit-slice micro processor.
Once again, a software orientated solution allows sophisticated but flexible processing on key shapes. In fact,
the circuit employed is a true shape pattern recognition
system that is able to make available the information on
size and shape of key at the end of the field to make it
ready for use at the start of the next. In this way lag
through the system is kept to a minimum.

The 2900, therefore, provides information on horizontal and
vertical position, as well as horizontal and vertical size,
but it will be noticed that this information is not fed
directly to the arithmetic unit as would be expected.
Instead the data is fed via a LSI-11 to allow complex
computations to be performed to cope with problems of
maintaining aspect ratio as the foreground camera pans the
key off the screen. Similarly, it is the LSI-11 that computes
the intrusion of talent into the key area and ensures the
inserted picture continues to remain stable at all times.

The Switcher Interface

Figure 6 shows the switcher video interface. The DPE 5000
being a framestore device can be set to have apparent
'negative' video delay. This makes the video interface
trivial for virtually any switcher. The inclusion of EFF/1,
EFF/2 and EFF/3 outputs into the auxiliary bus allows re-
entry effects such as the classic "hall-of-mirrors" created
by re-circulating a compressed picture.

An interface that allows control from the handle bars and
switches of the switcher itself, rather than the 5000 control
panel, would, at first sight, appear to be more complex, but,
in fact, the successful auto key system ensures that this interface is also trivial.

It has already been shown that the auto key circuit is able to
accurately track a key shape. Now, clearly there exists inside
every switcher effects package a wipe shape that if displayed
on a monitor would be the shape of the pattern selected. If
this signal is fed to the 5000 auto key circuit then, as
different patterns are selected, or the handle bar moved to
modify the shapes, the 5000 compressed image will automatically
follow.

Thus the simple matter of connecting the pattern generators of
the three effects amplifiers to the 5000 ensures total integration with the switcher. Push on or push off, squash on or
squash off, box wipes, circle wipes and many more complex
functions are possible from the control area of the switcher
itself.

This concept has now been proven to be most successful on the
majority of switchers in use today. Since no modification is
necessary to the switcher itself other than bringing out the
wipe shapes to the rear panel, it has been found possible to
interface the unit to several control rooms, each with a

different switcher, on a time shared basis.

SYSTEM EXPANSION

Although an effects system has been described, no attempt has been made to present all of the effects possible. In view of the difficulty of describing visual effects with the written word and the now commonplace use of the system by broadcasters, whether in sports, drama or light entertainment, it is felt more appropriate to concentrate on the framework of the system with particular emphasis on how the software orientation gives rise to field expansion capability.

System expansion takes two forms, firstly the refinement of controls and existing features in the light of users comments and, secondly, the addition of new effects and facilities.

Refinement to the basic system has been an ongoing involvement with all customers since the first deliveries in late 1977. Modifications to the control panel, border generation and auto key system have all been carried out by replacing program PROMs on site.

Work to extend the effects available in the machine has also been continuing with three major additions now available and more to be announced in the future.

AUTOSEQUENCE

The power of the LSI-11 has ensured that the 5000 is delightful to control but in some circumstances just six preselect buttons have been found to be a limitation. Users have identified a need for a non-volatile memory system able to store whole series of effects for later recall.

Accordingly the Autosequence unit was devised. This is able to remember any sequence of effects on floppy disc for replay at any time.

One of the advantages of including an industry standard mini-computer in the system is that all the normal computer peripherals are available for use. Thus Autosequence was able to employ a conventional mini floppy disc unit as the memory medium.

The Autosequence system allows the Operator to store any sequence of effects created with the DPE 5000 control panel. The sequences are stored on the mini floppy disc in such a way that complete interchange with any other similarly equipped 5000 is possible. In this way Directors and Producers can carry their chosen library of effects from studio to studio. This is clearly important if identical effects are required on each of the different programs in a series.

The control panel and disc unit are shown in Figure 7. It will be seen that the control panel is divided into two halves 'USE' and 'PRESET'.

The system is designed to allow a number of sequences to be recorded on one disc. Each sequence is given a number which is set up before the sequence is recorded. To replay the sequence the number is selected on the NEXT SEQUENCE display and the START button is pressed. The 'SEQUENCE IN USE' display always shows which sequence is running. Of course the 'NEXT SEQUENCE' display can be updated at any time to be ready for the next cue.

A simple thermometer display shows how much disc has been used. One disc gives sufficient space for approximately 2 minutes of movement. In practice this playing time is found to be more than adequate due to the very large difference between elapsed time and effect movement time.

During a show the required sequences can be preselected one at a time and replayed on cue. Alternatively, the powerful running order feature can be used. Once the order of sequences has been decided, this can be pre-programed into the Running Order Store. This is effectively a list of sequence numbers and the order in which they will be used.

Thus, during a show the only action required by the Technical Director is to press the START button on cue. Each time the button is pressed the next sequence in the order will be replayed.

The system is also able to accept a cueing signal from another device. This makes the simple interface between the 5000 and a computer tape editing system.

PICTURE REVERSAL AND TUMBLE

An effect commonly produced by film opticals is that of reversing or producing a mirror image of the picture. The flexibility of the software approach has enabled such facilities to be retrofitted to the 5000 by adjusting the program in the 6800 and the LSI-11.

Modifications to the 6800 were associated with setting appropriate co-efficients and parameters to cause the address circuits and algorithms to operate in reverse. Two additional states were added to the commands understood by the 6800. These were instructions covering the reversal of the picture and about which axis the reversal was to take place.

Simple reversal of the picture is interesting but, once again, if the power of the LSI-11 is used this simple effect can be 'brought to life'. By allowing the reversal to take place many times in succession at the same time as modulating the width or height of the picture, the illusion of a picture spinning is produced. If the modulation is that of a cosine law, and the period of rotation is reduced at the start and finish of the effect, the appearance of a picture on a board rotating is indistinguishable from the genuine article. Similarly, when alteration in picture mean size and position is permitted at the same time as spinning the image the illusion of a tumbling picture is complete.

No additional controls were necessary to accomplish this new feature, re-programing of the Intel 8748 in the control box allowed additional modes of existing controls to be used.

AUTO LINK

The majority of users of the DPE 5000 have more than one studio or edit bay in their facility. In view of the simple switcher interface it has become normal for several control heads to be used with the effects unit so that the machine may be allocated to different switchers as demand dictates. The control heads are left permanently installed in the various switchers, the appropriate head being plugged into the 5000 as required.

Clearly, manual plugging and unplugging of heads is not an optimum operational system and, therefore, a simple control routing switch known as Auto Link was developed. However, the distributed computation between the control head 8748 and the main LSI-11 allows a much more sophisticated concept with the possibility of multiple picture operation.

MULTI LINK

As the popularity of digital effects has grown the use of just one machine on a time-shared basis with several control heads becomes inefficient. For this reason there has been a natural progression towards the equipping of facilities with more than one 5000 unit. Normally, of course, each machine is used with its own control panel but the multi link concept permits the user considerable flexibility by allowing the interlinking of up to four DPE 5000 units with up to four control heads.

The multi link system allows machines to be coupled together on the occasions that multiple picture manipulation is required and then returned to independent operation immediately afterwards.

The concept is shown in Figure 8. The system comprises three parts. The switching unit, the assignment panel and the selection panel.

The assignment panel contains an array of 4 x 4 switches. Columns represent machines and rows control panels. These switches are mechanically interlocked so that it is impossible to select two control panels controlling one machine, but with this one exception all other possible permutations and combinations are allowed. Thus, by pushing the appropriate buttons any single machine can be controlled by any single control panel or any 'group' of machines can be controlled by any single panel. For example, one panel can take control of four machines, or one panel control two units and another panel control the remaining two units.

This approach obviates the necessity of tying up expensive multiple picture manipulation equipment with a single switcher when such facilities are only occasionally needed. However, the advantages of the multi link approach do not stop at system utilization.

During the initial experiments with INTELLECT it was found that the algorithms giving the best picture quality used all the information available in the store, irrespective of how small was the compressed image finally produced. Using multi link one complete framestore is available for each image allowing 'optical' quality to be maintained.

Since multi link allows the images to be combined in the switcher, as opposed to the framestore, each picture can be treated like any other camera source. Thus total flexibility of dissolves, wipes and mixes is available. Similarly, existing key priorities in the switcher can be used to enable one picture to be apparently moved either in front or behind another. The use of a 'mix' in this mode is particularly spectacular.

The provision of four auto key computers in the four machines can allow four independent background pictures to be automatically keyed into a foreground camera if four different coloured chroma key shapes are used.

Perhaps the most important advantage of the concept is, however, the power that the four individual computers bring to simplifying the controls.

Figure 8 shows multi link as including an extra 4" x 4" control panel to augment the normal 5000 control head. This panel is shown in Figure 9 and it will be seen that it is merely a control selection system. The four buttons are used to indicate which machines are being commanded by the control head at any given time.

Each LSI-11 stores all the information concerning the moves to be made by its own machine. Once control has been assigned to an individual control panel the entire operation of multiple picture manipulation is performed using the conventional preselect buttons on that panel. This is made possible by multi link ensuring that each of the locations is able to store independent data for all machines.

Each of the four buttons on the selection panel refers to an individual 5000 unit. Buttons may be pushed together or separately. A normal sequence of operation for a four picture shot would be to enter the desired moves one at a time into a preselect location by taking control of each machine in turn with the selection panel. The final composite effect can then be viewed by merely selecting all four machines and then operating the preselect facility normally. A single operation of the chosen preselect location will cause pictures from all four machines to move.

Of course control from the switcher control arms is possible by inter-facing the various machines to different effects desks. 'Push off' 'pull on' effects can be created from a single control arm by inverting the key sense in one of the LSI-11's by means of the key invert switch on the control panel.

The only hardware required to accomplish multi link is the switching unit and of course the various switches themselves. The rest of this system expansion is achieved by software modifications alone.

CONCLUSIONS

The background leading to a new generation of software orientated digital video equipment has been outlined. The importance of this novel approach in the field of video effects has been discussed and an equipment, the Quantel DPE 5000 Digital Production Effects system, representing the first in this new line of devices, has been described.

In the goals set for the DPE 5000 the ability to create optical effects in real-time with no loss of picture fidelity ranked equal with the demand for ease of control and the facility for field upgrade of existing equipments.

The machine has two primary uses - the first associated entirely with creative work to produce spectactular effects on the screen and the second associated with corrective work where shots incorrectly formed at the time of origination can be modified in post-production.

The control and upgrade concepts have been fully covered but, in spite of this paper being devoted to the field of video effects, no attempt has been made to rigorously describe all of the effects possible and no demon-stration of the optical qualities of the machine has been given. It is felt that their descriptions must, by definition, be left to the visual rather than the written medium. Fortunately, the regular use of the equipment every day by Broadcasters in North America gives an excellent chance of seeing the equipment at work. However, it is ironical that the best measure of quality is gained by the number of observers who when viewing flawless material may be quite unaware that the original has been modified by the machine.

The success of the software approach has been demonstrated in the description of the major new effects and facilities that are being added to the equipment in the field, largely by software changes alone. It is felt by the design team that the limits of software upgrade have yet to be explored, and thus the expanding world of digital video effects for the broadcaster is assured.

After graduating with a Bachelor's Degree in Electrical Engineering from Manchester University and a Master's Degree in Electronics, Richard Taylor joined the Research Labs of EMI. It was here that he originally became involved with broadcast television when he designed the first live automatic registration system for color cameras.

Mr. Taylor later moved on to manage the Video Processing Department where he was responsible for a number of novel designs, among which were unmanned airborne reconnaissance systems, digital standards convertors and image processing systems for infrared cameras.

Subsequently Mr. Taylor left to take up the post of Managing Director of Quantel Limited. Quantel specializes in Digital Video Products, and during his time with the company, Mr. Taylor has seen built up an impressive list of unique equipment for the broadcaster.

Fig. 1. INTELLECT video processing system.

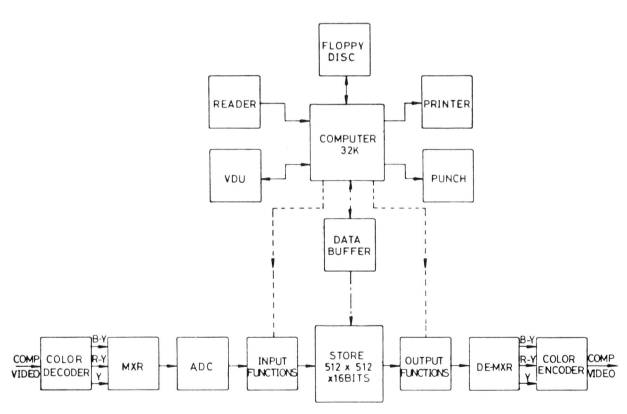

Fig. 2. INTELLECT basic block diagram.

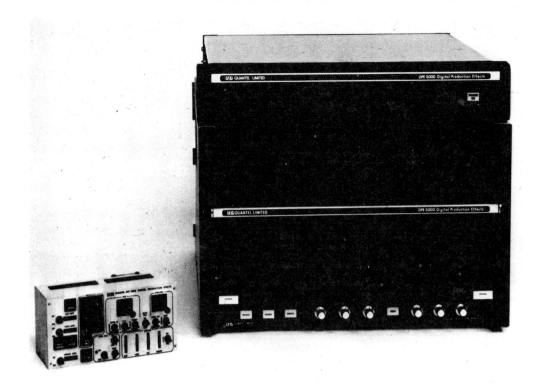

Fig. 3. The DPE 5000 system.

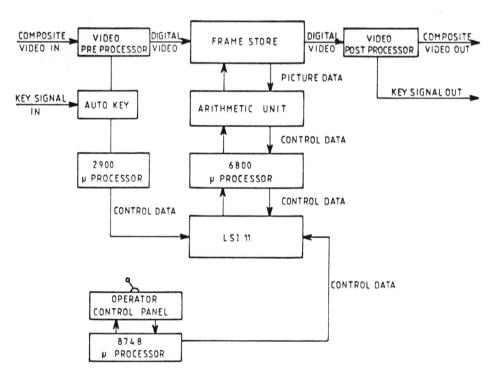

Fig. 4. DPE 5000 basic block diagram.

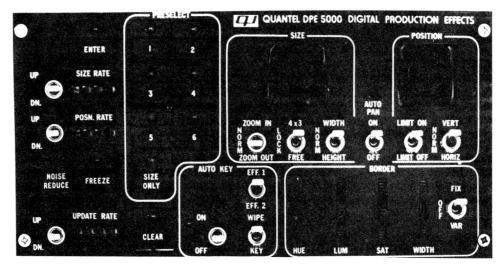

Fig. 5. Operator's control panel.

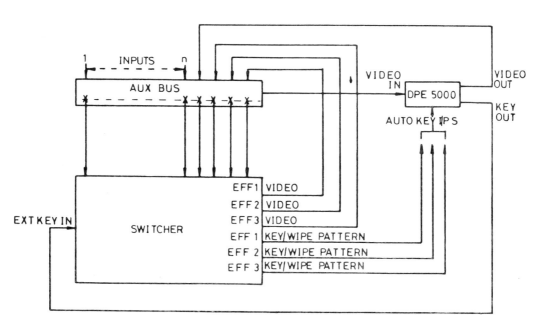

Fig. 6. DPE – switcher interface.

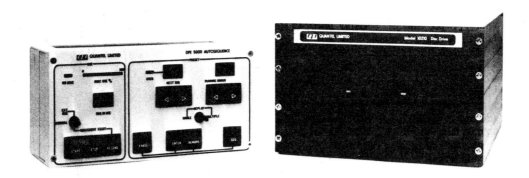

Fig. 7. Autosequence control panel and disk unit.

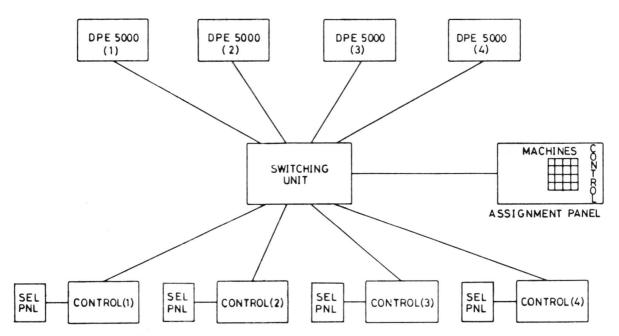

Fig. 8. Multi-link control system.

Fig. 9. Multi-link control panel.

The Use of the Computer in Animation Production

Dr. Edwin Catmull and Dr. Alexander Schure
New York Institute of Technology
Old Westbury, New York

ABSTRACT

NYIT has assembled a team of computer scientists, video technicians and animation artists for the express purpose of generating images and animation of professional broadcast quality.

The facilities include many computers, framebuffers, 2-inch videotape machines, sophisticated computer graphics equipment and a post-production video studio. The central piece of equipment is the "frame-buffer," a memory which stores an entire rgb picture, has a video output port and a port for random access by computer.

NYIT has undertaken a considerable software effort to make that hardware useable in a production environment. The programs developed thus far give us the capability to "paint" backgrounds, to color animated figures, create special effects, combine images, change scanned-in images, and digitally synthesize or modify a broad class of images. Our focus has been on 2-d animation. Having made substantial gains in solving problems in that area we are currently adapting the programs for production.

The researchers have paid considerable attention to the technical problems of aliasing, color control and image quality. In addition they are now focusing on 3-d animation.

The work has not been without difficulties. Digitally synthesized pictures can take from 15 seconds to 2 minutes to create using a general purpose computer. In addition, once a program is developed, it must be moved out of a research environment and into a production one.

The NYIT system of hardware and software has been successfully used to make an animated film, some test commercials and animated sequences to demonstrate the power and versatility of the system. We have been able to produce some astonishing results.

INTRODUCTION

The New York Institute of Technology has created a facility for producing animated films and video tapes using computers, special computer graphics equipment, a post-production video studio and a team of artist, researchers and technicians. This paper describes the facility and its research and production activities. There are two parts to the facility: the Computer Graphics Lab and the Video Center which is a full post-production video studio.

The goal of the Computer Graphics Lab is to assemble hardware and software systems capable of producing cost effective educational and commercial films of high quality with the unusual visual effects made possible using digital techniques. Recently NYIT produced a half-hour educational film "Measure for Measure" which successfully mixed conventional animation with computer assisted animation using two different methods. In addition, in the last few months several test commercials have been made and aired.

THE VIDEO CENTER

The Video Center is a fully operational studio with five two-inch IVC9000 VTRs, three Ampex 2000B VTRs, Ampex HS100C video disc recorder, two Vital switchers, telecine, several color cameras and the necessary supporting video and audio equipment. The VTRs and mixers have interfaces to a PDP11/34 computer to allow for computer assisted editing. A new mixer will soon be installed that will have digital mixing control and event memory of our own design. The IVC9000 recorders have been modified for a 700 millisecond lockup and the unique capability of recording one frame at a time for animation.

The Video Center is connected to the Computer Graphics Lab by a multichannel CATV system. Both digital and video signals can be passed between the two centers and it is possible for the Computer Graphics Lab to control the video equipment in the Video Center.

THE COMPUTER GRAPHICS LAB HARDWARE

The major pieces of equipment in the Graphics Lab are:

1. Framebuffers
   Each framebuffer is a 512x512 byte memory with a video port and an interface to computers which allow random access. Thus, a framebuffer can store a color picture which an artist can observe while using computer programs to modify the picture. We have a total of 22 framebuffers: 6 from Evans and Sutherland, 12 from Genisco, and 4 from Deanza. Framebuffers may be allocated in threes to give 8 bits each for red, green, and blue components. The framebuffers are the focal point of the software in the lab. All images to be recorded are assembled in the framebuffers.

2. Computers
   We have a VAX 11/780, PDP 11/70, 11/45, seven 11/34's, and various 11/35's and 11/04's for special functions. The 11/70 is our central time sharing machine. The VAX is a production recording machine which assembles pictures into framebuffers. The 11/45 is devoted to real-time line drawing hardware. The 11/34's each have an 88 megabyte disc, a real-time refresh vector display and tablet. They are used as standalone graphics stations for artists and researchers.

3. Scanner
   The Deanza framebuffers have a unique processor that digitizes a video signal and performs frame time image process-

ing in the resulting digital image. There is also a slower
video digitizer from Spatial Data for scanning in still
artwork.

4. Film recorder

   We have a Dicomed D48 color film recorder. With this we
   can record the contents of framebuffers onto 35mm movie
   film with high precision.

5. Video recorder

   There is an IVC9000 VTR (in addition to the five in the
   Video Center) which is capable of single frame recording
   and is under control of the 11/70.

6. Line drawing displays

   For real-time interactive 3d graphics we have E&S Picture
   Systems I and II. For 2d graphics we use the Three Rivers
   GDP which is capable of drawing an immense number of short
   vectors. There are also six Tektronix 4014's for less
   demanding applications.

7. Other

   We have digitizing tablets, Barco monitors, and other typical support equipment.

THE SOFTWARE

   Over the past four years the staff of the Computer Graphics
Lab has developed several proprietary software systems and programs to use the various equipment to make animated sequences.

1. Paint

   This system allows an artist to paint by using a pen and
   tablet and watching a color tv monitor. Developed by Dr.
   Alvy Ray Smith, the paint system is versatile and easy to
   use. It is in full-time use by artists who have no technical training. The artists are able to control a virtual
   paint brush in position, color, and size. Every artist who
   has used the system has been able to maintain his own style
   while producing pictures at a faster rate.

2. Scan-and-paint

   The drawings of conventional animation are normally copied
   onto acetate and colored by hand. Dr. Garland Stern has
   developed a system call Scan-and-paint where the drawings
   are scanned into a framebuffer, painted with the aid of a
   computer, merged onto backgrounds painted with the Paint
   system, and recorded directly onto videotape or film. Its
   primary advantage is that one can color drawings far faster
   using the computer than can be done by hand.

3. Tween

   A system called Tween has been written wherein drawings
   that have been traced in can be played back in real-time,
   colored automatically, and for simple figures intermediate
   drawings can be created from extreme poses.

4. Utilities
   There is a large body of special effects routines for generating pans, zooms, blurring, highlights, distortions, etc. Several high quality commercials have been created using these routines.

5. Three Dimensional objects
   Programs have been developed for displaying images of three dimensional objects made of polygons, ellipsoids, and bicubic patches. The objects can be manipulated in real time on a Picture System or rendered as solid surfaces into framebuffers.

THE ARTIST AND THE COMPUTER

While we have stressed to artists that the computer is nothing more than a new tool, some have felt threatened. When they use the programs some have tried unsuccessfully to make the computer do exactly what they do on paper. Other artists have embraced the new tools and quickly produced polished and satisfying images.

Some of the artists who use the system have no technical background at all and do not need it. The goal for any software put into production is that an artist be able to use it naturally with minimal training and only need to go to an operator for assistance if needed.

CURRENT RESEARCH

The research staff is focusing on several areas:

1. 3d
   A major effort is directed toward the creation, manipulation and rendering of 3d data bases so that images appear realistic. These techniques make possible some powerful tools for storytelling.

2. Scanning
   At times our system is used as if it were a "digital optical printer." We must, of course, be able to scan in images from film or videotape with minimum loss of image quality. This requires precision equipment, compensation programs for any intensity nonlinearities or illumination variation, and image enhancement programs.

3. Faster processing
   While digital processing is very general, it is sometimes slow. We are currently building a very fast microprogrammable processor/frame buffer system. One important criteria for the processor is that it be easy to program.

4. Sound
   Digital audio equipment has just been acquired to go with an array processor (Floating Point System AP120-B) to give us a capability for digital synthesis and manipulation of sound.

SUMMARY

By using the digital framebuffer and the general purpose computer we have put together an image making system with great capability. The NYIT system of hardware and software has been successfully used to make an animated film, some commercials, and animated sequences to demonstrate the power and versatility of the system. We have been able to produce some astonishing results.

Edwin Catmull graduated in 1975 with a Ph.D. from the University of Utah. His dissertation was on the computer display of curved surfaces. He is currently director of the Computer Graphics Lab at NYIT.

Alexander Schure holds the degrees Master of Arts, Doctor of Philosophy, and Doctor of Education, from New York University. He received an honorary Doctor of Engineering Science from Nova University. Prior to assuming the presidency of New York Institute of Technology in 1955, Alexander Schure was president, concurrently, of Crescent Electronics Corporation, New York City, and the New York Technical Institute (1948-1955).

Some Experiments in Television Graphics and Animation Using a Digital Image Memory

Richard G. Shoup
Xerox Palo Alto Research Center
Palo Alto, California

Introduction

This paper describes an experimental digital video system which can be used for interactive creation and manipulation of simple, cartoon-like graphics and animated imagery. The videographics system (known informally as "SuperPaint") was designed and built at Xerox in 1973 as an experiment in computer imaging and digital picture composition. Since then, it has been further developed as a computer graphics research tool and used for a variety of experiments in television graphics and imaging.

Most recently, the system was used extensively during the NASA Pioneer Venus mission for visualization of spacecraft maneuvers during the encounter with Venus, for showing activities of the scientific experiments on board and for illustration of early results obtained. A live video feed from the system was provided during the mission for closed-circuit viewing by the press at NASA Ames Research Center. Graphics and animation created on the system were also used in numerous network and local television news broadcasts.

The System

The system consists of a digital *image memory* (frame buffer) which holds 480x640 pixels (8 bits per pixel), a data tablet and pen, a minicomputer and several digital disk drives for picture storage. Fig. 1 shows an overall block diagram. When viewed at this level, the system is quite similar to more recent frame buffer drawing systems[1,2,3]. However, a novel image memory architecture and user-oriented software (see below) provide considerably more graphical power and flexibility than the typical frame buffer configuration.

Output from the system is via RGB and NTSC standard video signals. Hard copy output on ordinary paper is also available via a laser-driven xerographic color printer[4].

Operation

All drawing, editing and animation are done and all commands are given to the system via the pen and tablet. The operator (often, but not necessarily, a graphic artist) need not have any programming or computer experience. On a standard RGB color monitor directly in front of him, the operator sees the picture on which he is currently working (the "canvas"). On another monitor to his left, the operator sees a second picture (the "control panel") showing a palette of available colors, a variety of brush shapes and sizes, and icons representing various picture editing operations which he can invoke (Fig. 2). Colors and brushes are selected and operations are initiated by pressing down lightly on the pen when it is positioned over the desired item -- much like pressing a button. At the top of the control panel are three slider scales indicating the hue, saturation, and brightness of the currently selected color.

On an adjacent computer terminal screen to his right, the operator is occasionally prompted or advised with messages such as "Please specify a window..." or "Touch color to be replaced...". By utilizing these messages, a naive operator can safely explore the system and easily discover many of its features for himself. There are no other buttons or keys and the operator is required to type on the terminal keyboard only when a name is needed to reference a stored picture.

Graphics and animations may be composed in a variety of ways. Items may be drawn ("videopainted") by the user directly into the canvas picture. Prepared art work or other material may be input to the system via a conventional vidicon camera or other video source. The incoming video can be masked with a rectangular window and threshholded to create a high-contrast version. The resulting subimage can then be used just as if it had been drawn. Text can be added utilizing digitally-stored fonts. Parts of previously created pictures can be recalled and inserted, as can computed or synthetic imagery from other computer programs.

Objects or areas in the picture may be scaled up or down in size, moved, copied, overlaid, combined or changed in color, and saved on disk for future use or erased. See Fig. 3. Also provided are automatic drawing of straight lines of variable width and filling in of closed outlines with a selected color. Line endpoints and positions of moved or copied objects may be automatically constrained to grid points of a specified spacing. This allows easy creation of charts and graphs, etc., and alignment of items in a picture.

Each of the 16 available colors in the palette may be independently adjusted in terms of its hue, saturation, and brightness using the slider scales at the top of the control panel. As the operator adjusts a color, the palette and all areas in the canvas picture containing that color change simultaneously on the displays. By selecting the label to the left of the sliders, the operator can change the meaning of the scales to represent the red, green, and blue components of the color.

Implementation

The image memory is arranged in two identical banks (corresponding to the control panel and the canvas pictures), each 480x640 pixels by 4 bits per pixel. MOS shift registers are used and the memory continually recirculates in synchrony with the scanning of the raster. Fig. 4 shows one of these two banks with the recirculation path highlighted. Every memory cycle is a read-modify-write cycle. Thus, the contents of the memory are changed by switching multiplexer 1 at an appropriate time during scanning of the image.

In addition to controlling the disks, the tablet and other peripherals, the CPU (presently a Data General Nova 800 16-bit minicomputer) can also provide a data stream to the image memory. This stream is supplied in synchrony with the raster scanning and usually represents a paint brush image or a cursor. Data from the CPU is run-length encoded in X (along the scan line) and is expanded by hardware in the image memory. This enables the relatively slow CPU to provide this stream in real time for simple brush shapes and cursors. Overlaying the brush image on the canvas picture is accomplished simply by switching only multiplexer 2 at the appropriate pixel times. Note that since an overlaid cursor is never stored in the memory, no rewriting is necessary when the cursor moves.

Storing (painting) into the picture is done similarly by switching multiplexer 1. In order to accomplish the real-time brush overlay and painting functions, the multiplexer switching must be controlled at every pixel time by the value of the brush pixel. If the incoming brush pixel value is 0 (the background or "transparent" value), then the canvas pixel value is taken. If not, the brush pixel value itself is used. Thus, a brush or cursor can have arbitrary shape and will appear correctly over any background.

Digitized incoming video can be entered into the memory by switching multiplexer 1 to input 2. This is also under pixel-by-pixel control via the CPU data path, so that a brush or other image from the CPU can be used to "paint" parts of the incoming video into the canvas picture.

When a picture is loaded from a disk file into memory, it is transferred similarly by the CPU at a rate of about one runcode per scan line each frame time, with (optionally) only non-zero pixels being stored. Thus simple cartoon pictures can be brought into memory in only a few frame times, while very complex ones can take over 30 seconds.

In the design of the software, considerable attention has been paid to making the system natural and comfortable for the user. Note, for example, that fully half of the image memory is used solely to hold the control picture, thus giving it a similar visual appearance to, and equal stature with, the image being created. A symbolic visual interface is more appropriate to this graphical medium than giving commands by text item selection or by typing or button pushing. The control panel is, of course, itself a picture created and edited on the system. The "buttons" on the control panel can therefore be easily changed to accomodate improvements.

Also, the control picture dims to 1/2 brightness whenever the operator is expected to be directing his attention to the canvas. When selection of a control panel item is expected, a cursor appears and the control picture returns to full brightness as an added cue to the operator. If the operator changes his mind or acts inadvertently, any operation which has been invoked can be aborted and control returned immediately to the control panel by a single tablet stroke.

Animation

The value of movement in visual communications is great. Fortunately, even very simple motion in an image can produce a vastly more effective visual communication than a still image. If we do not require elaborate or complex motion in our images, then a simple, highly interactive form of animation can be effected using the color table hardware often included in frame buffer systems.

The *color table* is a small fast memory (usually a bipolar RAM) which holds the red, green and blue values associated with each possible pixel value (Fig. 1). During scanning, each pixel value is used to address the color table and the resulting color component values are passed to the D/A converters. The CPU can change the color definitions stored in the color table during vertical or horizontal blanking times.

In the present system, a form of limited but very effective animation is provided which relies upon changing the colors of objects hidden within a single picture[5]. Several views of an object are placed at successive positions along its path of motion, each in a different color number (pixel value). See Fig. 5. Initially, all the views are hidden by setting the color table so that each of these pixel values displays a color identical to the background color. The animation effect is then created by manipulating the color table definitions so as to turn on or reveal the hidden objects one at a time in sequence. Notice that successive images can be different in shape and size so that much more than just simple translation of the object is possible. Furthermore, several objects or areas can be in apparent motion simultaneously. Successive images cannot overlap, however.

The operator can manually step through the animation or he can set a speed via the tablet and allow the cycling to proceed continuously. Instead of suddenly changing from background to foreground color, smooth transitions are made between steps in the animation by interpolating in RGB color space over several frame times. The degree of interpolation depends on the speed of the animation. This softening is essential for a pleasing visual effect at all but the fastest speeds. The software also makes it possible to paint into the picture while the animation is running.

Currently, only 10 colors are used for cycling and animation and 6 are static or background colors. It is worth noting that 10 animating colors are quite sufficient for a wide variety of simple cartoon-like animated graphics. This means that motion in the image must be effected in 10 or fewer steps. Our application here is not continuous, story-telling animation, but rather simple self-contained graphics such as shown below.

Application

Artists and non-artists alike have responded positively to using the system. Most people quickly adapt to the videographic medium and are able to create interesting drawings and graphics with only a few minutes of experience. The medium acts somewhat like an amplifier -- it expands greatly the range and scope of both the trained graphic artist and the non-artist.

Figs. 6a-d show examples of animated graphics by artist Damon Rarey for use during the Pioneer Venus mission. Like all the figures below, these pictures were created on the system and printed by a laser xerographic printer.

Limitations of the system are numerous and apparent after some use. Most annoying, of course, are the jagged edges often present in the picture due to the limited resolution and lack of softness of the digital medium. Techniques now exist for eliminating these quantization effects[6,7], but utilizing them fully in a highly interactive system is beyond the capabilities of this hardware. Other desirable features not present in the current system include: multiple overlays (like a cartoonist's cels), the ability to deal with full-color natural images as well as flat color, smooth scaling (zooming), and a more general animation capability.

Acknowledgements

The author would like to thank Damon Rarey for his enthusiastic use of the system and for many important comments and suggestions. Thanks are also due to Bob Flegal and Alvy Ray Smith for their early work on this system and for numerous useful ideas and discussions.

References

1. A. R. Smith, "Paint," Tech. Memo., New York Inst. of Tech, Old Westbury, New York.

2. H. K. Regnier and L. J. Evans, "Interactive Computer Graphics in the Broadcast Environment," Proc. International Broadcasting Convention, London, 1978.

3. J. T. Kajiya, I. E. Sutherland, and E. C. Cheadle, "A Random Access Video Frame Buffer," *Proc. IEEE Conf. on Computer Graphics, Pattern Recognition and Data Structure*, 1-6, May 1975.

4. *6500 Color Graphics Printer*, Xerox Corp., Rochester, New York.

5. R. G. Shoup, "Simple Animation by Changing Color Definitions," to appear in *Proc. ACM Siggraph Conf.*, Aug. 1979.

6. R. G. Shoup, "Some Quantization Effects in Digitally-Generated Pictures," *SID Symposium Digest*, 58-59, May 1973.

7. F. C. Crow, "The Aliasing Problem in Computer-Synthesized Shaded Images," *Comm. ACM 20:*, No. 11, 799-805, Nov. 1977.

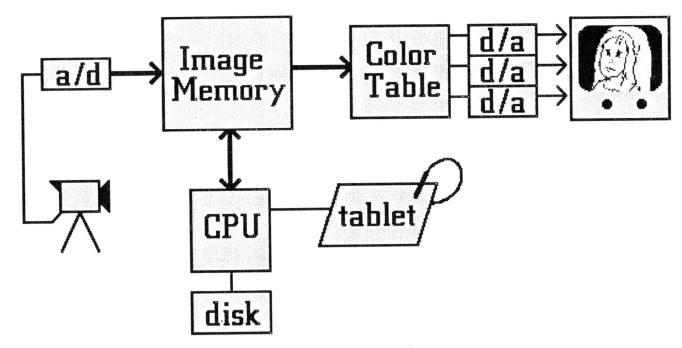

Fig. 1. Overall system block diagram.

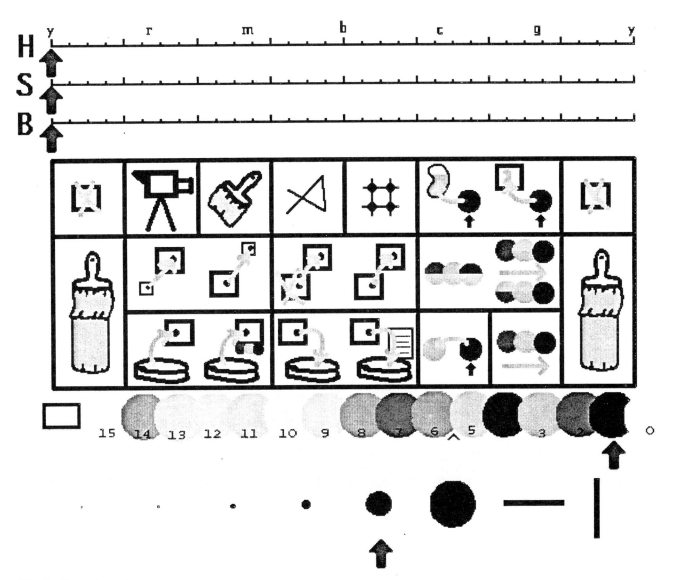

Fig. 2. Control panel.

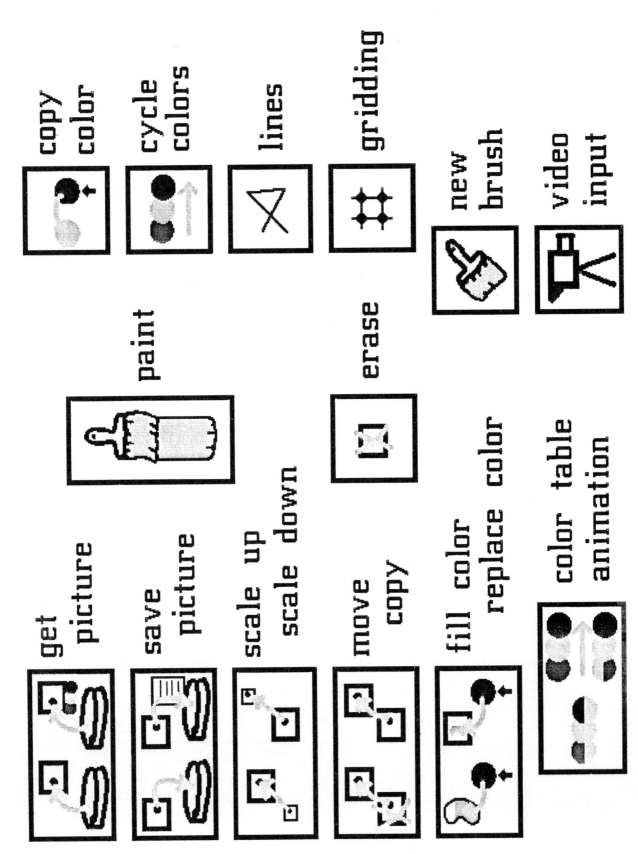

Fig. 3. Control panel icons.

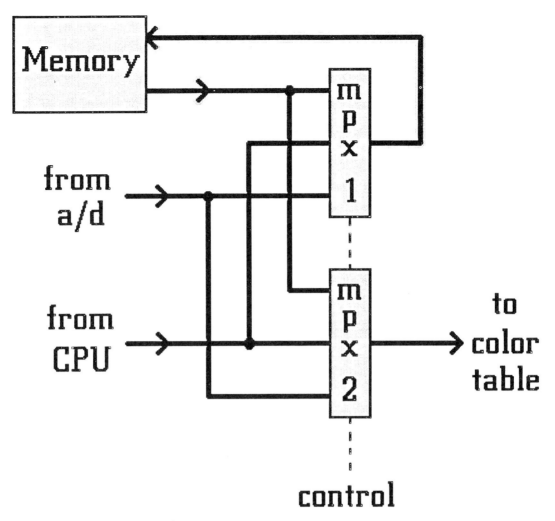

Fig. 4. Image memory block diagram.

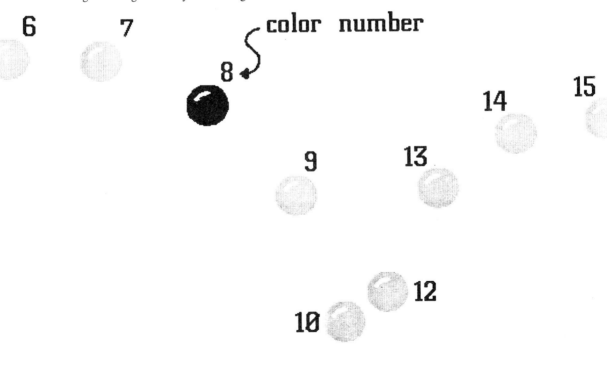

Fig. 5. Color table animation.

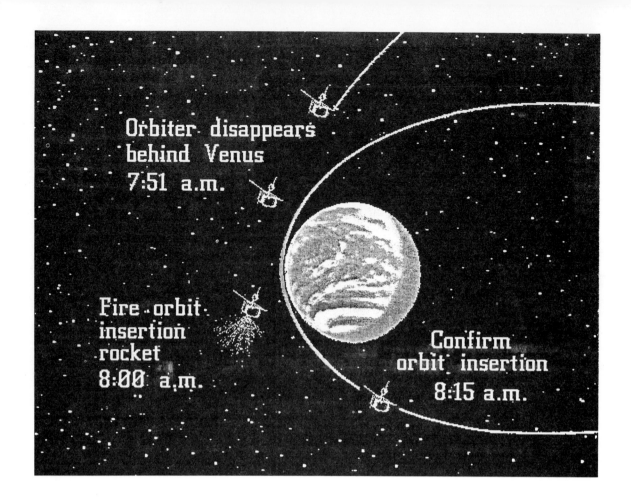

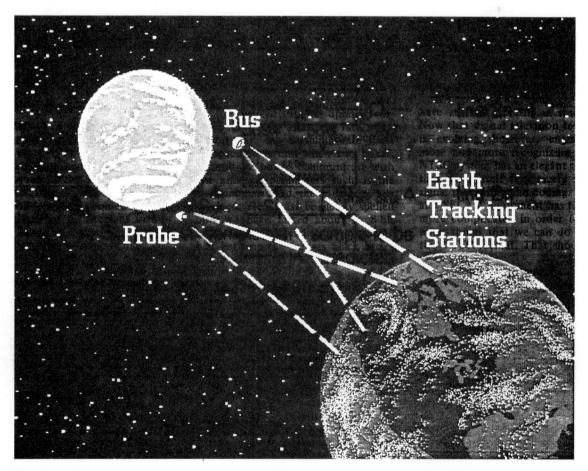

Fig. 6a-d. (Facing pages) Pioneer Venus videographics.

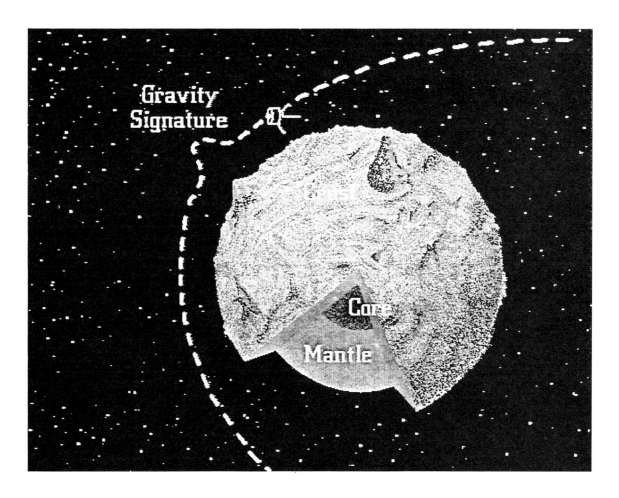

Richard G. Shoup was born in Pittsburgh, Pa. in 1943. He received the B.S. degree in Electrical Engineering in 1965 and the Ph.D. degree in Computer Science in 1970, both from Carnegie-Mellon University in Pittsburgh.

Dr. Shoup is currently active in computer science research at the Xerox Palo Alto Research Center. His interests include digital video graphics, parallel machines and personal computing media. Before joining Xerox in 1971, he was with the Berkeley Computer Corporation in Berkeley, California.

Color Graphics and Animation by Mini-Computer

Noboru Asamizuya and Tatuo Futai
Sony Corporation
Tokyo, Japan

Currently, color graphics display units are used to communicate certain kinds of information, such as computer data and broadcast election results. In such cases animation outputs are more suitable for correct, immediate and effective information communication than still pictures. If a device for easy production of animations is available, it can be useful in broadcasting and education.

With this goal in mind, we have developed a realtime animation generator for use with the standard NTSC television system. This equipment generates realtime pictures from computer data and can vary the pictures in realtime through order from a joystick or a light pen. A picture is formed through the composite layering of basic trapezoidal patterns. This reduces the computing task of the computer, allowing comparatively small computers without mass storage to be utilized.

FEATURES OF REALTIME ANIMATION GENERATOR

The picture area of a monitor is divided into a grid of m x n picture elements. According to data from the computer, these elements are colored, so that a picture can be created. Three methods have been developed to date and put into practical use:

1. Dot method: A series of data signals are sent out for each element in order, from left to right and top to bottom. The memory corresponds to the total picture on an element by element series of signals.

2. Symbol method: A previously stored symbol (combination of elements) is withdrawn from the memory at any time and inserted into the picture.

3. Stroke method: A basic pattern is defined by a set of parameters, which are freely adjustable. As the parameters are redefined, the pattern changes shape. The pattern can be located anywhere in the picture.

Method 3 is most suitable for the realtime animation generation (with the standard television scanning) because its picture composition is flexible and the picture data requirements for one picture can be reduced.

The realtime animation generator we developed adopts the trapezoid shown in Fig. 1 as the basic pattern in Method 3 and adds the concept of a priority level to the basic trapezoid figure. The priority level indicates which pattern is superimposed upon which: that with a higher level is superimposed upon that with a lower level. Except in the case of overlapping patterns with identical priority levels, there is no confusion on the part of the block as to which pattern it represents, unlike previous models.

The features of our realtime animation generator can be summarized as follows:
  Low data requirements for each picture.
  Processing task reduced through direct, numeric
    coordinates to represent each pattern.

The introduction of the priority level prevents
confusion in the case of overlapping patterns.

These features reduce storage requirements for the picture data, since only the parameters necessary for pattern modification need by processed. Thus, realtime animation can be achieved even with small computers without mass storage.

CONSTRUCTION OF THE REALTIME ANIMATION GENERATOR

The block diagram of this equipment is shown in Fig. 2 and the following is a brief explanation of the main blocks.

1. Trapezoid Pattern Data Buffer (TPDB)

The parameters of the basic patterns are stored in the data buffer, arranged by the vertical order of the upper edge. An interface unit transfers these from the computer into the buffer memory. Thirty frame per second motion is possible, but to reduce computer usage time, for complex pictures variable speed motion (15 fps, 10 fps, etc.) can be effected, maintaining the impression of regular motion, but with less demands on the computer. For still picture display the data buffer contents need not be changed. The capacity of the data buffer is 256 trapezoid patterns.

2. Trapezoid Pattern Data Register (TPDR)

In the trapezoid display, the Y coordinate of the upper edge (SY) indicates the display initiation and that of the lower edge (EY) indicates the termination. When the Y-line counter reaches SY, the data of that trapezoid is transferred from the TPDB and when the Y-line reaches EY, that trapezoid's data in the TPDR is erased. During the period the trapezoid's data is in the TPDR, the horizontal points are calculated through interpolation by two adders, for each horizontal sweep. The TPDR can store up to 32 patterns simultaneously.

3. Color Buffer (CB)

When the TPDR calculates the horizontal start and end points through interpolation (SX and EX), the color buffer memorizes these points and the color information for the segment in between. The required memory size for the buffer is equal to the product of the number of priority levels involved multiplied by the number of elements in one horizontal line. Two color buffers are required because the data for one scanning line is made up and written into one color buffer while the data for the preceding scanning line in the other color buffer is fetched out and the line is displayed.

4. Composite Layering Control Circuit

This circuit consists of priority level flip-flops and composite layering gates. When the start and end points memorized in the color buffer are reached, the flip-flop changes state, the composite layering gate then selects the highest priority level available and applies this color information to the succeeding block signals.

5. Y-line Counter

With each horizontal sweep, beginning at the top of the picture, the Y-line counter counts down one line.

6. TV Sync Generator

The unit can be locked to an external sync signal; it also contains within itself all timing signals necessary.

OPERATION OF REALTIME ANIMATION GENERATOR

Let's proceed from the point where the picture data has already been entered into the buffer memory TPDB.

Figure 3 shows the flowchart of the write operation into the CB. Counters I and J, which are the address pointers of the TPDB and the TPDR respectively, are set to 0 and the Y counter to "239" as the initial setting during the vertical interval period. The following takes place during each horizontal scan. First, the 32 trapezoid information memories in the TPDR are checked in sequence to determine whether they are empty or full. (B(J)=1 indicates the memory is full; B(J)=0 indicates that it is empty.) If the memory is empty, the TPDB buffer memory is asked whether there is a pattern which begins with the next horizontal scan; if so, then those trapezoid parameters are transferred into the TPDR.

Secondly, the data in all the active memories is transferred into the CB, to be displayed in the following horizontal scan. As described above, it is during this period in the CB that interpolation calculations are performed for each trapezoid, to determine the start and end points SX and EX for the next horizontal scan. Now, let's take a look at this again, in more detail.

A. Write into CB (Color Buffer)

When the TPDR memories are examined during the horizontal scan, to determine whether they are empty or not, the empty memories are not used. In this case, the buffer is asked whether there is a trapezoid which will start in the next horizontal scan. Since there are 256 memories in the buffer memory (from 0 to 255), the I<256 refers to whether all memories have been checked or not. However, since the trapezoid parameters are listed in the buffer file by the order of their upper edge (the highest first, the lowest last), there is no need to check all these memories at once; if the memory just asked did not contain a pattern to start in the next horizontal line, neither would any of the succeeding memories due to this vertical ordering. By the end of the frame, though, all 256 memories will have been checked; when I=256, this is the signal that no more pattern data is in the buffer, and the TPDR will no longer request such, upon finding an empty memory in the TPDR.

After the thrity-two memories have been examined during one horizontal line, the TPDR is read again, during the succeeding horizontal scan. If B(J)=0, it goes on to the next. If B(J)=1, an end point marker locates SX(J) and EX(J), together with color information (C(J)), as it is written into the CB of the designated level (L(J)). To determine the next end points, the interpolation calculations are performed with equations (1) and (2) below, for such time as EY(J) is less than Y (the period until the Y-line counter reaches the value of the Y coordinate of the bottom edge of the trapezoid.)

$$SX(J) = SX(J) + \triangle SX(J) \ldots \text{formula (1)}$$
$$EX(J) = EX(J) + \triangle EX(J) \ldots \text{formula (2)}$$

These calculations are performed in the two adders shown in Fig. 2.

When the Y-line counter value reaches that of EY(J), the trapezoid has been completed, and the memory B(J) returns to zero, emptying the trapezoid's data.

When the Y-line counter reaches zero, it indicates the completion of the operations for one picture. As the Y is above zero, "1" is subtracted with each horizontal scan.

B. Read from CB

Figure 4 shows an example of composite layering, or superimposition of patterns. Trapezoid A has a priority level of 0, trapezoid B of 1, and C has a level of 2. Figure 5 shows how the CB would process horizontal line Y_i: each trapezoid's signal is separate and indicates the start and end points and color information. When a start or an end point is detected, the flip-flop (LF) switches, and the composite layering gate selects the color with the highest priority level. At the end of the horizontal line, during the blanking signal, the flip-flop is reset to zero.

The composite layering operation is performed as follows. The level 0 figure is superimposed on the background picture, the level 1 figure on the level 0 figure, and thus the layering is continued, producing the output shown in Fig. 5.

The introduction of the composite layering produces the advantage of free picture composition without any consideration of interference among figures, and furthermore, reduces the load of the processor for producing picture data.

The composite layering circuit outputs only a limited number of hues, so the color mapping ROM is used to expand upon this selection, before sending the signal to the D/A converter and the NTSC color encoder, to render it a color TV signal.

OUTPUT PICTURE

Figures 7-1 to 7-4 show the pictures outputted from this realtime animation generator. Figure 7-1 is a kaleidoscope pattern, composed of about 96 trapezoids. The colors of the figures change and the figures rebound when they collide with the wall. Figure 7-2 shows an example of a graphic display composed of about 120 trapezoids. The position and shape of the graph can be changed with an external input (joystick). The electric charge transfer process of a CCD (Charge Coupled Device) was modeled for an animation composed of about 40 trapezoids as shown in Fig. 7-3. The operation of the frame transfer system CCD video camera was illustrated with the animation in Fig. 7-4, composed of about 110 trapezoids.

The size of each computer program used is as follows:

Figure No.	Program Size	
7-1	1540W	
7-2	2747W	1W (Word)
7-3	720W	=16 bits
7-4	1138W	

To execute a program such as this, an additional memory size of 1300 to 2700 W is necessary for the basic routines (figure definition and input/output routines) and the picture data area.

Output Signal
    NTSC Television signal
      Images per second: 30 frames
      Interface: 2:1
      Scanning line: 525 lines/frame
Displayed Picture
    Effective address number
    Scanning line: 480 lines/frame
    Picture element: 256 (512)/scanning line
    Picture element clock: 5 (10) MHz
Sync Signal Generator
    Usable with internal sync or external sync by Genlock
Memory Used
    Type: RAM
    Data buffer memory: 256W (1W = 78 bits)
    Data register: 32W (1W = 84 bits)
    Color buffer memory: 8K byte (16K byte)
D/A Converter Section
    Independent 64 colors
    2 bits for each of R, G and B channels
Logic Elements Used:
    Approx. 300 pieces of TTL, SSI and MSI
Dimensions and Power Consumption
    430mm(W) X 700mm(D) X 450mm(H), 200VA
Processors Utilized
    HP-21MX: 16KW memory (1W = 16 bits)
    Input/output device: Paper tape reader, TTY

Figure 6 shows the realtime animation generator, processor and monitor. The cabinet at the lower section of the left rack is the realtime animation generator and the one above it is the interface for the processor. The right side rack contains the processor, HP-21MX system, to control the generator. The display is on the left.

CONCLUSIONS

An animation such as the one in Fig. 7 is somewhat simple compared with one produced manually, but the advantages of the generated animation are as follows.
    The time required for producing an animation is short.
    The production cost is not expensive.
    Specification changes can be done easily.
    The animation can be recorded directly on a videorecorder.
    There is no deterioration of the picture over time due to
        color fading or frequency of use.

The animation described above is one of the applications of this device. The application fields can be enlarged as follows with the development of the necessary software.
    Picture generator for professional utilization at broadcast stations
        Realtime graph generation
        Pattern generation for program titles
        Animations for infant and education programs
    Educational applications
    Graphic display for computers
    Driver training simulators
    Game machines

Since the pictures are somewhat crude, due to the limitations of a 256 block horizontal grid, we are currently in the process of increasing resolution to 512 blocks. Also, we are studying means of relaxing the necessity of ordering the trapezoids vertically, to reduce the hardware configuration requirements.

ACKNOWLEDGMENTS

We express our appreciation to Mr. M. Kikuchi, Chief of Sony Corporation Research Center, and Mr. H. Yoshida, General Manager, Research and Development Division, Video Products Group, for giving us this opportunity to study and develop this device, and to Mr. S. Sakoda, Manager, for his prominent technical guidance. Also, to Mr. M. Morizono, Managing Director, Video Products Group, for the chance to present this report at the SMPTE Conference.

REFERENCES

1. Machida, Kutsusawa, et al: "Colour Figure Output Device for Computers," Study Data on Picture Display System issued by Television Institute, July 1973.

2. Morito: "Trend of Graphic Display," Television, Vol. 29, Aug. 1975.

3. Mita: "Trend of Graphic Display," Television, Vol. 29, Jan. 1975.

4. Suzuki: "Graphic Display," Television, Vol. 29, Dec. 1975.

5. Suzuki: "Broadcasting and Information Process Technique," Monthly of NHK Technical Research Center, Vol. 20, Aug. 1977.

6. Kutsusawa: "Computer Animation," Shingaku Monthly, Vol. 60, May 1977.

7. Suzuki: "Computer Animation," Television, Vol. 28, April 1974.

8. Hosaka: "Computer Graphics," Sangyotosho Co. Ltd., 1974.

9. J. George: "Computer Graphics," Siggraph - ACM, Vol 11, Feb./Mar. 1977.

10. Carl Machover, et al: "Graphics Display," IEEE Spectrum, Aug. 1977.

Noboru Asamizuya entered the Sony Research Center in 1970 to work on CAD system for digital IC's. After this, he carried out research and development on digital video image generators. Currently in the Research and Development Division of the Video Products Group, he is engaged in the development of a video system for broadcast use.

Tatuo Futai entered Sony in 1968 and worked on the development of electronic calculators. Since 1973 he has been in the Sony Research Center, developing image simulators and computer graphics hardware.

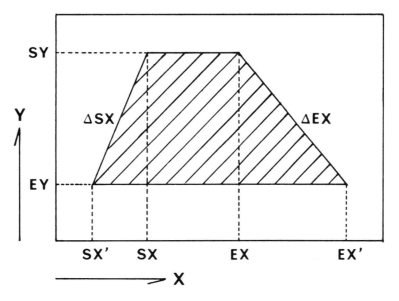

Fig. 1. Basic pattern of the system

SX : X coordinate of left end point of upper edge
EX : x coordinate of right end point of upper edge
SY : Y coordinate of upper edge
EY : Y coordinate of lower edge
SX' : X coordinate of left end point of lower edge
EX' : X coordinate of right end point of lower edge

$$\Delta SX : \frac{SX - SX'}{EY - SY} \qquad \Delta EX : \frac{EX - EX'}{EY - SY}$$

Definition of basic pattern parameter

SX, EX, SY, EY, SX, EX . . . . . . trapezoid pattern
C . . . . color information
L . . . . priority level

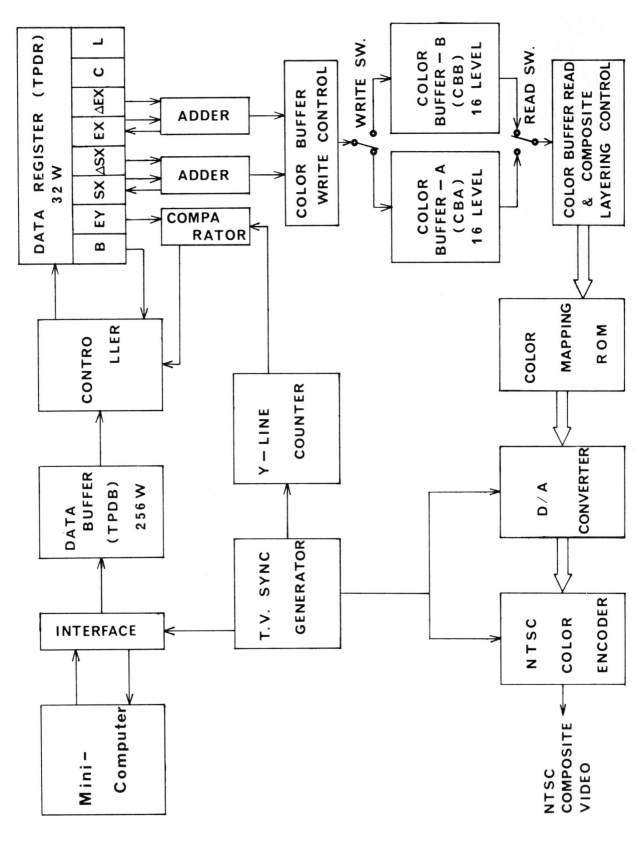

Fig. 2. Block diagram of the system.

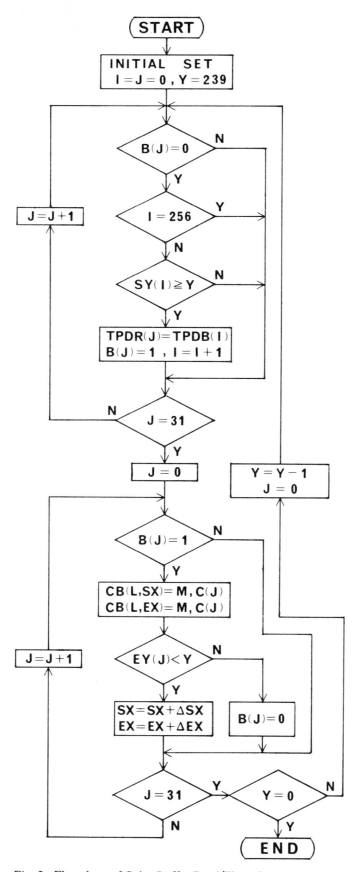

Fig. 3. Flowchart of Color Buffer Read/Write Operation

    I: address counter of data buffer (TPDB)
        $0 \leqq I \leqq 225$
    J: address counter of data registor (TPDR)
        $0 \leqq J \leqq 31$
    Y: Y-line counter, $0 \leqq Y \leqq 239$
    M: end point marker

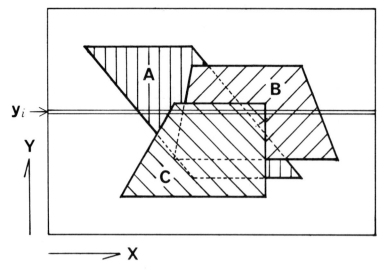

Fig. 4. An example of composite layering.

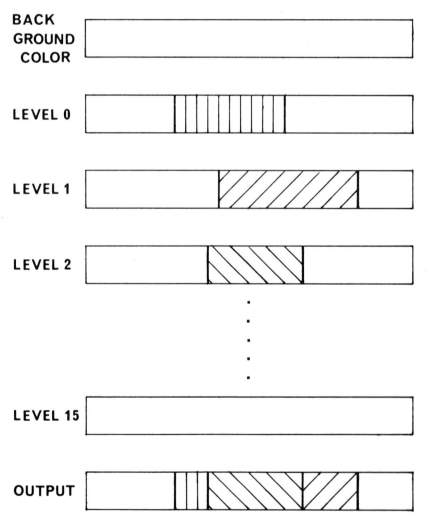

Fig. 5. The output at horizontal line Y_i of Fig. 4.

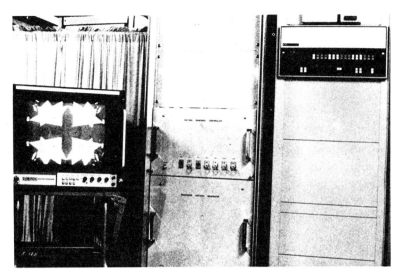

Fig. 6. Photograph of the system.

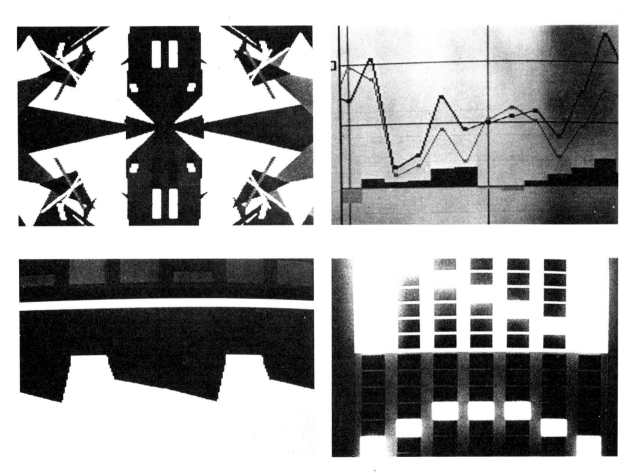

Fig. 7. Output picture from the system.

The Mosaic Keyer

Shigeru Jumonji
Japan Broadcasting Corporation (NHK)
Tokyo, Japan

INTRODUCTION

The use of microcomputers is becoming widespread in recent times, so much so that we are said to be in the age of microcomputers now. It is small wonder, then, that the microcomputer is finding its way into broadcasting equipment also. The mosaic keyer to be described here is a compact TV pattern generator unit for video special effects using a microcomputer (MC6800) (Fig. 1). This unit divides the TV raster into 64 elements each in the vertical and in the horizontal directions (in all, 4096 elements) and controls the writing in each of these elements by means of a microcomputer.

CONFIGURATION

The mosaic keyer consists of the MEK6800DII kit as the basis, and this consists of the central processing unit (CPU) and a keyboard, and the video control circuit having a 12K-byte program memory and 12K-bit picture memory, and a fader unit. A Peripheral Interface Adapter (PIA) (MC6820) is used as the interface, and a photo-tape reader and a cassette tape recorder are used as the peripheral devices. The block diagram of the mosaic keyer is shown in Fig. 2.

The mosaic keyer first stores the picture information in the picture memory and then reads it out in the predetermined sequence to form the picture signal. In order to carry out the writing in and reading out of the data bits independently of each other, a data bit is written in the memory during the blanking period while it is read out during the display period. The PIA on the CPU side supplies the writing-in horizontal address code giving the horizontal position, the writing-in vertical address code giving the vertical position, and the data to be written. The clock generator uses the half-duplex (HD) signal to generate the reading horizontal address code and the reading vertical address code that divide the raster into 8 to 64 horizontal and 8 to 64 vertical elements. These outputs are fed to SW_1 (Fig. 2).

The video signal generator part consists of the picture memory corresponding to the data of the colors red, green, and blue (RGB) the latch circuits, the gate circuits for eliminating unwanted signals during the blanking period, and an encoder. The switching of the data sent to the picture memory is controlled by the program through the PIA.

Provided in this unit is a fader lever whose position is read out by the computer by means of a 12-bit A/D converter.

The selection of the mode among the modes possessed by the mosaic keyer (to be described later) and the selection of the pattern within each mode is made by means of the 24 keys on the keyboard. This keyboard is also used during the designing of a pattern, etc.

The mosaic keyer gives the various effects by altering the address information, the input picture data, and the read/write control information supplied to the picture memory. The switching of these data and the different types of information are described below.

(1). Address Information

The TV signal consists of one part which appears on the TV screen (the display period) and another part which does not appear on the TV screen (the blanking period). During the display period, the contents of the picture memory in the mosaic keyer are specified by the address sequentially as 1, 2, 3, ..., according to the scanning pattern as shown in Fig. 3. On the other hand, during the blanking period, the address will be specified by the CPU. The switching between them is made by the horizontal blanking level signal (HBL) in SW_1.

(2). Read/Write Control Information

This information decides whether a new data bit is to be written in the picture memory or the data bit is to be read out from the picture memory. This signal will normally be in the Read state so that the data bit in the picture memory can be read out. The data bit in the picture memory will be changed in the Write state, for which the mosaic keyer has two types of timings for generating the pulse that changes the state into the Write state. One of these is the timing of generating the pulse during the HBL period. During this timing, the picture element data bit whose address is specified by the CPU will be updated.

The other type of timing involves generating the pulse during the display period, in which case one write pulse for each picture element will be generated. This write timing is generated when the sequential address is being specified by the scanning signal in the display period. Hence, the timing of the address specification and the write timing will always be simultaneous. In this timing, the data bit is read out immediately after writing the new data bit into the memory. In other words, the write data in the duration of the picture element specified by the address will remain the same.

The use of this timing permits the entire picture memory data to be updated within 1/60 s (one field).

Summarizing the above, the timing during the HBL period will be used when the data bit is to be written in the picture memory irrespective of the scanning signal; on the other hand, if the data bit is to be updated in accordance with the TV scanning signal, then the timing generated within each element will be used (SW_3).

(3). Input Picture Data

The input data can be either the ones supplied by the CPU or R, G, B signals decoded from the NTSC video signal (SW_2).

FUNCTION

The mosaic keyer realizes the following functions by appropriately arranging the various data in the picture memory:

(1). Animation Mode (Fig. 4)

This is the mode in which a moving tile pattern is generated on the TV screen; simple animation patterns can be generated. The sequence and the color of the tiles to be displayed will have to be predetermined. (It is possible to store 16 types of animation patterns.)

(2). Key Mode (Fig. 5)

The wipe key signals for scene changeover are generated in this mode. Using this key, one can produce a unique effect in which the tiles can be replaced one by one while changing the scene. In this mode, 13 types of patterns are available by the use of the CPU program, and three other types of patterns can be designed by the user freely.

(3). Video Mode (Fig. 6)

In this mode, the NTSC video signal will be changed into a color picture in a tessellated pattern. If, for example, a person's picture is displayed in this mode, then a picture in rough large tiles will be obtained. Since it is easy to alter this mosaic picture depending on the picture movement, it is possible to obtain a very effective picture by synchronizing with the rhythm of the music, etc. The color of each tile will be automatically selected as one of the colors of the color bars closest to the original color.

(4). Masking-off Mode

This mode gives a key signal which is used to mask off input letters line by line. The computer discriminates the positions of each line of letters on a TV raster and stores them into the program memory. In this mode, a TV raster is divided into 4096 blocks (64 horizontal, 64 vertical).

The speed of changing the tiles in the above four modes is controlled by the fader lever operated manually.

PROGRAM

(1). Memory Map

The memory map of the mosaic keyer unit is shown in Fig. 7. The addresses 0000-0127 and 2000-24FF (hexadecimal notation) are allotted for the program, while the addresses 2500-4FFF are allotted for the picture data. Addresses 4000-4001 are used by the fader data, and addresses 4010-4013 are used by the PIA data. The reason for separating the program area and the data area is to reduce the area occupied exclusively by one program and to use the 12K-byte storage area efficiently by separating the program into a data preparation program and a data reading program. The data bits in the data area can be referenced by either of the programs.

(2). Data Structure

The data bits sent from the CPU to the picture memory are output in the order in which they are propared in the program. The data bits that must be stored at this time are as follows:

(a). The address information giving the element of the TV screen in which the data bit is to be displayed.
(b). The color information about the color to be displayed on the screen.
(c). The pause information indicating whether the data bit is to be displayed after a pause or without pausing.
(d). The ALL information, in case the display is to be made over the entire screen as the background color rather than in a single picture element.

Storing the above four types of data requires 17 bits of storage as shown in

112

Fig. 8. Actually, 3 bytes (24 bits) of storage are kept aside for storing the data of each picture element.

(3). Reading Program

There are four modes of operation of the mosaic keyer unit, each of the modes being easily selectable by keyboard operations.

(a). Animation Mode

This is a mode in which the data bit in the data area is displayed in the sequence in which it is prepared. A maximum of 16 types of data can be stored in the data area. The top addresses of each of the frames are stored in the form of a table so that any of these frames can be called by means of a key on the keyboard. If the ALL data bit is present in the data brought from the data area, then the address information will be ignored and the color specified there will be displayed over the entire frame. This writing in for the entire frame in the picture memory can be made in one V period by using the writing timing within each picture element.

In case the data read out has the pause data bit, the fader position data will be read out, and the writing in will be made after pausing for a time corresponding to that fader position data. This pausing time duration is determined by the preparation of a loop by the program and the number of times that the loop is traversed.

(b). Key Mode

Since this mode is identical to the wipe mode being used commonly, the fader in this unit is related to the fader on the switching console. That is, in order to unify the FROM/TO relationships, the fader lever has been designed so that only the TO side picture will be displayed and all the segments will be white when the lever is in the position closest to the operator. The segments become dark one by one when the fader lever is moved to the position away from the operator. The segments become white one by one when the position of the lever is changed back.

(c). Video Mode

The data bits in the data area of the storage will not be used in this mode, but the effect is obtained by controlling the writing in timing. The input to the memory for the entire frame will be the data obtained by decoding the NTSC signal into RGB colors, the writing-in timing for these being the writing-in timing within each segment.

In the video mode, after the writing in is made within one vertical period, the writing in is inhibited for a time duration corresponding to the fader, and another writing in is made for one V period again, so that the continuous movement of the picture is made intermittent

(d). Masking-off Mode

The presence or absence of a character in each scanning line and the vertical and horizontal positions are read out from the PIA to control each element, thereby generating the key signal for masking off.

The above was a description of the outline of the reading program, the flow chart of which is shown in Fig. 9.

(4). Data Preparation Program

This is the program which prepares the data bits in the data area of the picture storage and has the following functions:

(a). Data preparation can be done by displaying a picture of the data bit on a color monitor. A cursor is displayed on the monitor, and the color of the cursor becomes the color data, while the address data bit is determined by the position of the cursor. Also, the pause data bit (and whether or not it is to be stored as data) is determined by the speed of switching of the cursor.

(b). Data bits can be corrected.

(c). The frame already loaded completely can be reproduced.

The above are the functions possessed by the data preparation program and all of these functions can be controlled from the keyboard. The flow chart of the data preparation program is shown in Fig. 10.

SUMMARY

The mosaic keyer is now in very wide use during the programs broadcast by NHK, such as music, news, and educational programs. Its versatility enables the effectiveness of each kind of program to be increased in a suitable manner. Many more applications can be foreseen for the mosaic keyer, and both hardware and software developments are in progress.

Shigeru Jumonji was a planner in the group which developed the mosaic keyer from 1977 through 1978. Since 1976 he has been a member of NHK's Engineering Operation Department where he is presently a senior engineer.

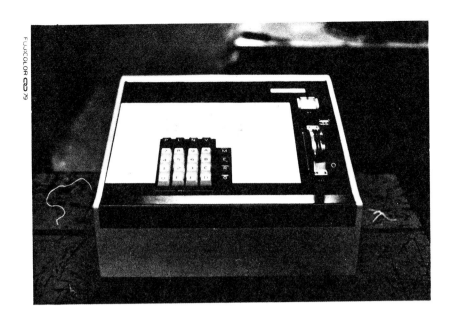

Fig. 1. The mosaic keyer.

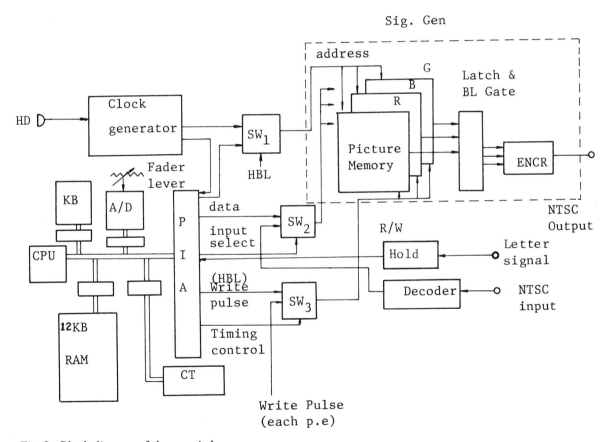

Fig. 2. Block diagram of the mosaic keyer.

1	2	3	4	5	 64
65	66				

Fig. 3. Picture memory.

Fig. 4. Animation mode.

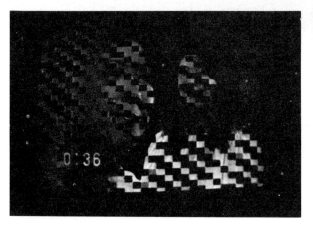

Fig. 5. Key mode.

Fig. 6. Video mode.

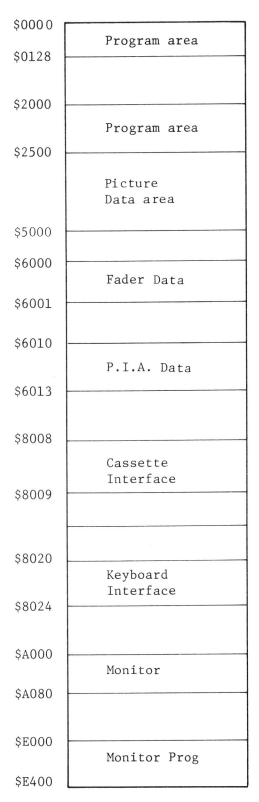

Fig. 7. The memory map.

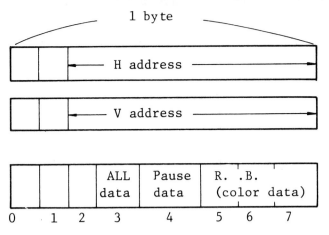

Fig. 8. The data structure.

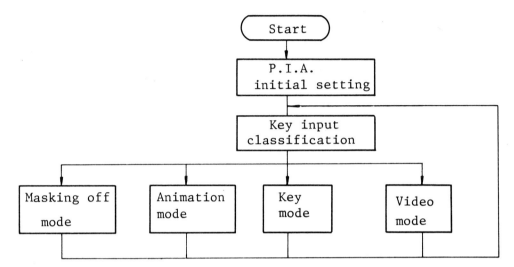

Fig. 9. The flow chart of the reading program.

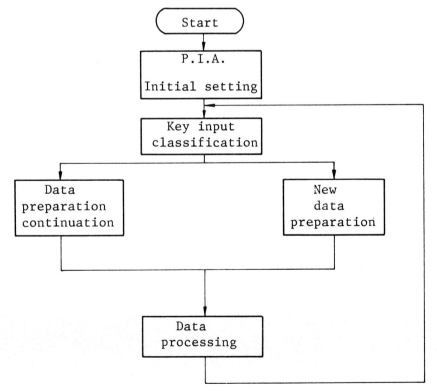

Fig. 10. The flow chart of the data preparation program.

Low Bit-Rate System for Digital Coding of the Television Signal

P. Rainger and P.A. Ratliff
British Broadcasting Corporation
London, England

INTRODUCTION

It is generally accepted that a bit-rate of about 100 Mbit/s is required for digital coding of high-quality television signals, using conventional linear p.c.m. Although such simple coding has many advantages in the television studio, it is grossly inefficient in terms of information-carrying capacity, and once the digital video signal leaves the studio, for distribution to local-area transmitters for example, it will have to compete with all manner of other digital signals in tomorrow's world of all-digital communications. The concept of universal, digital communication highways is fine, but the video signal is a greedy companion in comparison with the major occupant of these highways, the telephone signal. Similarly such video signals are greedy of digital storage media which will soon play a major role in studio-signal processing, and thus it is important to look at methods of coding them more efficiently. Of course, the final solution involves striking a balance between the cost of hardware required to effect a bit-rate economy and the cost of transmission or storage of the digital signal.

Ideally, the picture-quality given by the digital coding should be so high that the system is effectively transparent to the signal; then any number of separate systems may be connected in cascade without causing a progressive degradation of the signal. In practice, some loss of transparency may be tolerated where the impairment introduced is so small as to be virtually undetectable under conditions of critical assessment. However, if such an impairment is introduced by passing the signal through such a system once, it is important that this impairment does not build up to intolerable levels when the signal is subjected to passes through further systems. This requirement is essential for broadcast signals since they may well travel over several different transmission circuits and be recorded many times before reaching the general public.

With analogue processing, impairments almost invariably build up in successive stages, but with digital processing it is possible to devise coding systems which do not possess this short-coming. Digital systems may be arranged to have a certain basic precision which is the quality-determining factor, or degree of transparency of the system, but which can be substantially maintained however many stages of similar digital processing are employed. Such systems are said to be cascadable, and this paper is concerned with bit-rate reduction techniques for the video signal which fall into this category.

The digital transmission system currently under development by the BBC is designed for 625-line composite PAL colour video signals (to UK System I specification), and although this paper concentrates on this particular system, many of the points made are applicable to other television standards.

The methods currently employed in our system are removal of the blanking intervals, reduction of the sampling frequency to below the Nyquist criterion, and reduction of the number of bits/sample by differential p.c.m. (d.p.c.m.) (see Fig. 1). The system is designed to reduce the bit-rate of the video signal to about 30 Mbit/s, in order to fit a complete television package into the 34 Mbit/s level of the European digital multiplex[1].

BLANKING REMOVAL

Removal of the blanking intervals is, in principle, perfectly transparent, giving a bit-saving of about 24% without any loss of picture quality. In practice about 1 or 2% of the bit-saving may be sacrificed in order to transmit blanking format and control information. This is to facilitate the re-insertion of the blanking waveform at the receiving terminal, such that it is a close replica of that removed at the transmitting terminal, a particularly important feature where a mixture of analogue and digital processing exists. However, as digital technology spreads its inherent precision throughout the signal chain, there will be less need to take elaborate measures to reproduce, in a digital system, blanking waveforms distorted by previous analogue processes.

Assuming that such difficulties do not have any deleterious effect on the visible picture, it is our present interest to concentrate on those techniques which do involve processing of the active-picture signal and assume the blanking-interval processing to be transparent.

SAMPLING FREQUENCY

In the studio there is a growing demand for processing the composite video signal at a sampling frequency of four times the colour subcarrier frequency $(4 f_{sc})$, which is about 18 MHz for the PAL signal, and consequently well above the Nyquist sampling-rate criterion. Sampling at a frequency locked to the colour subcarrier has advantages for processing the composite signal, but because of the awkward relationship of subcarrier frequency to line frequency there is an 8-field cycle before the phase of subcarrier repeats at a given point in a stationary scene. Nevertheless, sampling at four times the colour subcarrier frequency gives rises to a sampling pattern which repeats once per picture, and is very close to the line-locked sampling frequency of $1135 f_H$. Thus digital processes for which line-locked sampling is preferable can be readily coupled to those preferring subcarrier-locked sampling[2] and, furthermore, PAL encoding and decoding may be effected without loss[3].

However, $4 f_{sc}$ sampling appears to further exacerbate the problem of efficient use of bit-rate for transmission or recording. Nevertheless, it is possible to cut the bit-rate by half by appropriate filtering and halving of the sampling frequency, provided that the phase of sampling of the original $4 f_{sc}$ samples is appropriately defined. This leads to the well-known sub-Nyquist sampled PAL system[4] and Fig. 2 shows a block diagram of the system with $4 f_{sc}$ interfaces.

The filtering employed only concerns the upper part of the video band (symmetrical about subcarrier frequency) over which the interfering or 'alias' components are normally produced with a reduction in sampling frequency to $2 f_{sc}$. In this band the **4** f_{sc} sampling structure is reduced to a $2 f_{sc}$ structure by taking alternate samples and averaging them with the interleaved alternate samples from the previous line; the reverse process is employed to regenerate $4 f_{sc}$ samples at the receiver. The filters, known as line-delay comb filters, confine the h.f. luminance to its predominant frequencies about multiples of line frequency, $n f_H$, and remove unwanted alias frequencies about $(n + \frac{1}{2}) f_H$. In addition, the chrominance information is transformed into uniform phase components of $(u + v)$ and $(u - v)$ on alternate lines, conventional u and v chrominance on every line being reconstructed in the decoder filter.

120

The reconstructed 4 f_{sc} signal is not identical to the original 4 f_{sc} signal and the main loss of transparency introduced by the 2 f_{sc} system is some loss of high-frequency diagonal luminance resolution. In the region of high horizontal frequencies, zero vertical frequency suffers no loss, but increasing vertical frequency suffers progressive loss to the point of total extinction at a frequency of 156 c/ph (cycles/picture height) on the 625-line system, which is equivalent to a horizontal frequency of 3.68 MHz in terms of spatial resolution. In addition there is some loss of vertical chrominance resolution (extinction at 156 c/ph) but this is of little consequence since the horizontal chrominance resolution is somewhat less than this in the normal PAL specification. Also a 12.5 Hz flicker can appear on horizontal boundaries between different coloured areas, but this is usually only visible on transitions between areas of certain highly-saturated colours. Even so, the subjective impairment introduced is judged to be very small (a loss of about 0.3 of a grade on the CCIR 5-point impairment scale[4]).

But now let us consider the effect of a number of sub-Nyquist sampling systems in cascade. If the system is to be useful, the impairment introduced by the first system must not significantly increase when the signal is passed through subsequent similar systems. Fig. 3(a) shows the essential elements of the sub-Nyquist sampling system and Fig. 3(b) a cascaded arrangement. Now, it can be shown that the effect of the system in Fig. 3(b) is identical to that in Fig. 3(a). This is true if the sample values from the second sampler are identical to those from the first sampler. Thus network G, a linear network with a given amplitude and phase response, must not generate intersymbol interference as Nyquist[5] determined for distortion-free reception of telegraph signals. The impulse response of G must be zero at all the sampling instants of the second sampler, except that corresponding to the time origin. Given that G is a network with uniform group delay it is sufficient to constrain its amplitude response $A(f)$ to be antisymmetric about half sampling frequency, f_s. Thus $A(f) + A(f_s - f) = 1$. When F_2 and F_1 are the normal comb filters associated with sub-Nyquist sampling, the response of G obeys this criterion and is of the form shown in Fig. 4(a). Its impulse response about the time origin is shown in Fig. 4(b) and it can be seen that this is zero at all other sampling instants. In particular, inspection of the impulse response at a time displacement D from the time origin, corresponding to the line-delay element in the comb filters, reveals a subsidiary peak at this point, as expected, but this corresponds to a point mid-way between the sampling instants; again the response is zero at the sampling instants. Thus the output of the second sampler is identical to that of the first sampler (but for a time delay) and no further degradation is introduced; the system is therefore cascadable.

There is still the small, but definable, loss of quality introduced by the first codec. It is worth considering whether this can be improved in any way. The cause of the loss is that the combining and separation of the samples in the comb filters is performed with orthogonally displaced sets. For example, consider the reconstruction of a 4 f_{sc} signal from adjacent lines of 2 f_{sc} samples as shown in Fig. 5(a). In order to remove the loss of spatial resolution the 4 f_{sc} samples must be reconstructed from samples in the correct spatial positions. This occurs if the samples are summed with those from the same line on the previous picture (i.e. across a 625-line delay) as shown in Fig. 5(b). With the PAL signal it is also fortuitous that the chrominance conditions are the same with a 625-line delay as with a one-line delay and thus for stationary pictures complete transparency is obtained.

Now spatial displacement has been traded for temporal displacement and hence a loss of resolution only occurs with picture movement, visible as a blur on moving edges. Thus an ideal system would be adaptive, employing picture delays in stationary picture areas and line delays in moving picture areas. Such a system can be expected to be effectively transparent provided that the transition from one type of filter to the other is not obvious, since the loss of resolution inherent with line-delay comb filtering is only just visible on critical stationary scenes, and movement reduces the accuity of the eye. However, both forms of filter are equally viable and so the transition could, if necessary, be made smooth, using a proportion **x** of one filter and a proportion $(1 - x)$ of the other, the value of x being under the control of a (rate of) movement detector.

It is seen that the sub-Nyquist sampling technique works well for the composite PAL signal but similar developments are possible for NTSC also. Unfortunately the simple form of sub-Nyquist sampling is not as transparent as for PAL, requiring 2-line delays to obtain the correct chrominance conditions[6], and hence giving double the resolution losses (assuming 625-line NTSC). Similarly, complete transparency to stationary pictures can only be obtained using 2-picture delays (for each comb filter), which would create even more serious movement problems. However, if the appropriate line from the previous field is used (line 312 in a 625-line NTSC system) a four-fold improvement in spatial resolution, relative to the 2-line delays system, is obtained with only half the movement blur of the picture-delays PAL system.

QUANTISATION

The third method of saving bit-rate is to reduce the number of bits/sample allocated to the signal. In linear p.c.m. coding, 8 bits are normally considered adequate for broadcast standards but a reduction in the number of quantising levels required may be obtained by employing differential p.c.m. techniques.

Fig. 6 shows the well-known d.p.c.m. coder configuration in which the difference between a prediction of the input signal and the input signal itself is requantised in a non-linear manner to achieve a reduction in the number of levels that have to be transmitted. Provided that the prediction of the input signal is reasonable, the difference signal has a highly-peaked distribution about the origin, and thus if the quantiser is arranged to transmit small differences with full accuracy but larger differences with progressively less accuracy, much of the picture information will be conveyed without loss. When loss of accuracy does occur the picture is highly detailed and the human eye is somewhat less critical of absolute coding accuracy. Thus a small loss of transparency is inherent in the d.p.c.m. process if bit-savings are to be made.

The problem of applying d.p.c.m. to the PAL signal is that the predictor must be effective not only for the luminance signal but also for the modulated chrominance[7]. Fig. 7 shows the spatial arrangement of sample sites in one television field for the 2 f_{sc}-sampled PAL signal, and also the colour subcarrier phase pattern assuming a plain coloured picture area. Because the eye is most sensitive to coding accuracy in plain coloured areas, the predictor is arranged to predict these correctly and thus the simplest predictor for the composite signal comprises the second-previous sample value. This has been used previously to provide a modest bit-saving with a 6-bit non-linear quantiser; the subjective impairment introduced was very small (a further loss of about one quarter of a grade on the CCIR 5-point impairment scale[4]).

Again the question arises as to whether this loss accumulates when the signal is passed through several d.p.c.m. systems in cascade. One may regard the transmitted difference signal of the first coder to be the true difference signal, A - B, plus an error E due to the non-linear quantiser. The first system decoder adds this to its predictor output B, which is the same as that in the coder, both being fed by previously transmitted information. Thus the final output of the first system comprises the sum of the system input, A, and the quantising error E. In a second similar d.p.c.m. system, the input becomes A + E and the true difference signal, or quantiser input, is now A - B + E, which by definition is an output state of the non-linear quantiser. Thus, provided that the non-linear quantiser is designed such that its permissible output states are given by the same-value input states (a condition satisfied by all sensible quantising characteristics), the output of the second quantiser is also A - B + E which is identical to that in the first system. Hence the output of each similar d.p.c.m. system in a cascaded network is A + E and the system satisfies our criterion of cascadability. (It is interesting to note that it would be theoretically possible under these conditions to omit the quantiser from subsequent d.p.c.m. systems in a cascaded network.)

Returning to the small loss introduced by the first d.p.c.m. system, it may be desirable to further minimise this loss with the same degree of bit-saving, or better still, with increased bit-savings by further reducing the number of permissible quantising levels. The simple predictor predicts steady-state colour correctly at the expense of a rather poor h.f. luminance response. This may be improved by adding a contribution from the previous sample provided that the chrominance prediction is corrected by contributions from further previous samples along the line. There is an advantage here that the chrominance bandwidth is less than that of the luminance. However much greater gains in prediction accuracy may be obtained if the prediction is spread into 2 dimensions by also using contributions from samples in previous lines. With the sub-Nyquist PAL signal there is no useful chrominance information in the previous line because of the v-axis switch, and two previous lines must be used to spread both luminance and chrominance predictions (Fig. 7). However, because of the necessity to form the prediction from previously-transmitted information, the prediction is still somewhat "one-sided" in its spatial frequency response. This problem can be largely overcome by introducing a 3rd dimension into the predictor, namely time. Samples in previous fields completely surround the one to be predicted and in this way it is possible to gain a prediction which is more uniform in its spatial frequency response.

In practice the weighting of the various sample contributions can be determined by computer from an analysis of a number of representative test pictures. The mean-square prediction error is minimised subject to the constraint that steady-state colour is predicted correctly, and a fixed temporal aperture is employed. This leads to the following conditions which must be satisfied (see Fig. 7):

1. the sum of the predictor coefficients equals unity,
2. the sum of the even coefficients minus the sum of the odd coefficients on even lines equals unity, and
3. the sum of the even coefficients minus the sum of the odd coefficients on odd lines equals zero.

Our optimisation is not yet complete but already the number of quantising levels has been reduced to 22 ($4\frac{1}{2}$ bits/sample) by using a 12-element 3-dimensional predictor (comprising 6 elements from two lines in each field) without perceptible loss of picture quality on stationary scenes. In fact it has been necessary to generate input-output difference pictures to be convinced that the d.p.c.m. is not quite perfect! Nevertheless, the problem of picture movement must be considered. Earlier work in monochrome had shown that previous-picture prediction gave rise to severe movement blur which was most objectionable on slowly moving edges, and thus an adaptive system would appear to be necessary as with comb-filtering. However, it was a pleasant surprise to discover that halving the time disparity and spreading the prediction contributions in both spatial and temporal zones proved to be a substantial mitigating factor. On slow moving edges additional quantising errors are virtually non-existent, and on fast moving edges, when quantising errors can be clearly observed on an error display, it was not possible to detect them on the normal decoded pictures. Lag could only be detected in the decoded picture under special conditions, for example when changing the direction of an artificial, high-speed, repetitive movement test card which had negligible restriction in the temporal aperture of the source. Thus it is possible to design d.p.c.m. systems with fixed 3-D predictors without encountering movement difficulties and which give a very high degree of transparency.

CONCLUSIONS

This paper has shown that despite the desire to use p.c.m. with a high sampling frequency for certain processes in the television studio and for general interfacing, it is possible to reduce the necessary bit-rate by a factor of about four for transmission and recording purposes without paying a significant penalty in terms of picture quality. Although efficient bit-rate reduction is based on a twice colour subcarrier sampling frequency $(2 f_{sc})$, it can be made virtually transparent to a $4 f_{sc}$ signal. Four times the colour subcarrier sampling frequency $(4 f_{sc})$ has been shown previously to be ideal for conversion from composite to component form and vice versa, and hence for changes of television standards. It is therefore possible to also make international exchanges using low bit-rate signals without incurring a severe loss of picture quality.

The sub-Nyquist sampling and d.p.c.m. processes involved have been shown to introduce, at worst, a small quality degradation, but one which does not accumulate if the signal is passed through a number of similar bit-rate reduction systems in cascade. At best, using more sophisticated implementation, the loss of quality introduced can be almost negligible, but the optimum solution to the question "how much bit-rate reduction?" will inevitably be a complex economic one; one needs to balance the cost of implementation of the techniques against the cost of the bit-rate they save and the quality of the signals they provide.

Although the discussion has been centred on the composite PAL signal and towards finding solutions which primarily meet the needs of the BBC, the UK, and hopefully the European Community, these solutions for PAL may also point the way for NTSC.

ACKNOWLEDGEMENTS

The authors would like to thank their many colleagues in BBC Research Department who have contributed to the work described in this paper and, in particular, to Messrs. A.H. Jones and D.W. Osborne who played an important part in its preparation. They also wish to thank the Director of Engineering of the BBC for permission to publish the paper.

REFERENCES

1. RATLIFF, P.A., Bit-rate reduction for high-quality digital television transmission. International Broadcasting Convention 78, IEE Conference Publication No. 166, September 1978.

2. JONES, A.H., Digital sound and television sampling-rate changing. EBU Review 163, Technical, pp 127-136, June 1977.

3. WESTON, M., A PAL/YUV digital system for 625-line international connections. EBU Review 163, Technical, pp 137-148, June 1977.

4. DEVEREUX, V.G., STOTT, J.H., Digital video: sub-Nyquist sampling of PAL colour signals. Proc. IEE, 125, (9), pp 779-786, September 1978.

5. NYQUIST, H., Certain topics in telegraph transmission theory. Trans. Amer. Inst. Elect. Engrs., 47, pp 617-644, February 1928.

6. ROSSI, J.P., Sub-Nyquist encoded PCM NTSC colour television. J. SMPTE, 85, (1), pp 1-6, January 1976.

7. DEVEREUX, V.G., Differential coding of PAL video signals using intra-field prediction. Proc. IEE, 124, (12), pp 1139-1147, December 1977.

Peter Rainger, C.B.E., B.Sc. (Eng.), C.Eng., F.I.E.E., is Deputy Director of Engineering, British Broadcasting Corporation. His degree is in Electrical Engineering (Northampton Engineering College, London University). He joined the BBC in 1951 and worked on film equipment, later moving to the field of magnetic recording and then signal-processing equipment of various types. In 1969 he became Head of Designs Department and was appointed Head of Research Department in 1971. Subsequently, he was promoted to the post of Assistant Director of Engineering and the Deputy Director of Engineering where he has responsibility for all research and development and the other specialist departments involved in capital projects throughout the BBC.

He was a member of the Electronics Divisional Board from 1969 to 1972. He has been the author of a number of papers presented to the I.E.E. and was awarded the Franklin premium in 1966.

He is chairman of the European Broadcasting Union Working Party V (New Technology). In 1964 he received the Royal Television Society's Geoffrey Parr Award for work on standards conversion and in 1973 he was made a Fellow of the Royal Television Society. In 1967 the Academy of Television Arts and Sciences presented him with an Emmy Award and in 1972 he was awarded the David Sarnoff Gold Medal by the SMPTE. In 1978 he was honored with the C.B.E.

P. A. Ratliff graduated from the University of Birmingham (England) in 1969 with a first class honours degree in electronic engineering. He was awarded a BBC Research Scholarship and remained at the University to study v.h.f. multipath fading and diversity reception techniques for mobile radio, for which he gained his Ph.D. degree in 1973. He then joined BBC Research Department where he has worked on both sound reproduction and digital video. He undertook a detailed study of subjective properties of the human auditory system which led to the development of the BBC Matrix H quadraphonic sound system. In 1977 he transferred to the Baseband Systems Section to manage the digital video bit-rate reduction project and he maintains a keen interest in subjective assessment of systems performance.

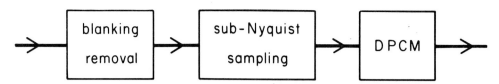

Fig. 1. Video bit-rate reduction system.

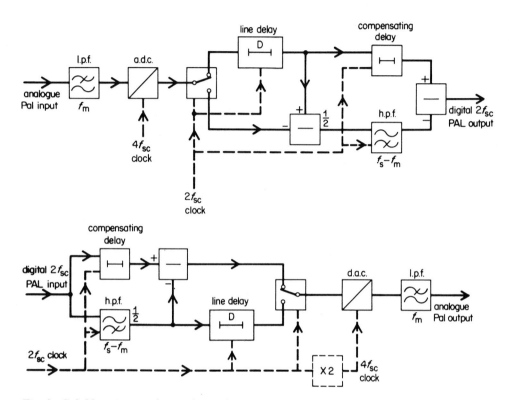

Fig. 2. Sub-Nyquist sampling codec with 4 f_{sc} interfaces.

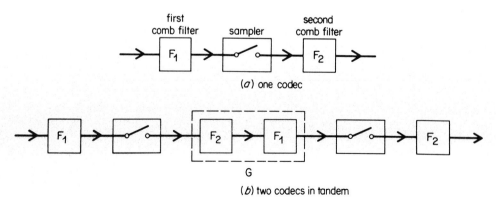

Fig. 3. Cascading of sub-Nyquist sampling systems.

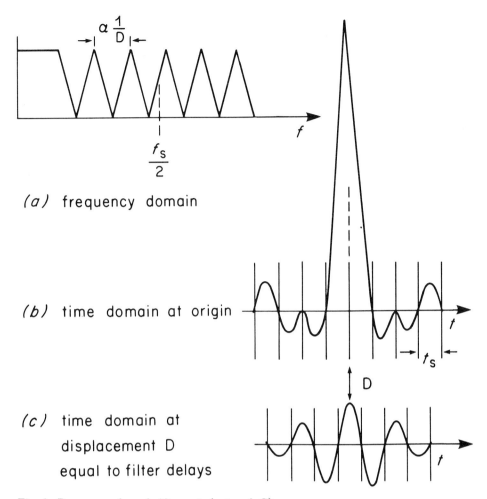

(a) frequency domain

(b) time domain at origin

(c) time domain at
displacement D
equal to filter delays

Fig. 4. Response of comb-filter pair (network G).

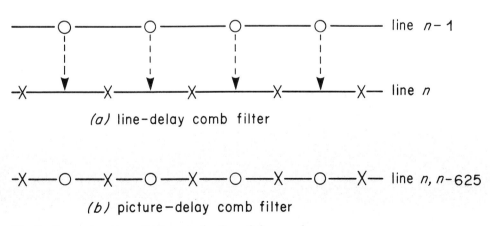

(a) line-delay comb filter

(b) picture-delay comb filter

Fig. 5. Reconstruction of 4 f_{sc} samples from 2 f_{sc} samples.

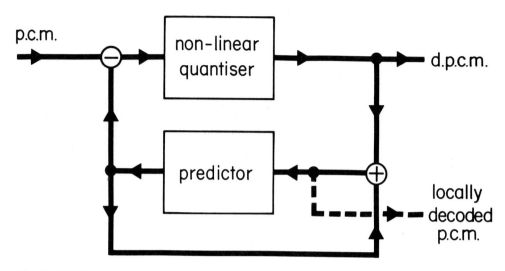

Fig. 6. DPCM coder.

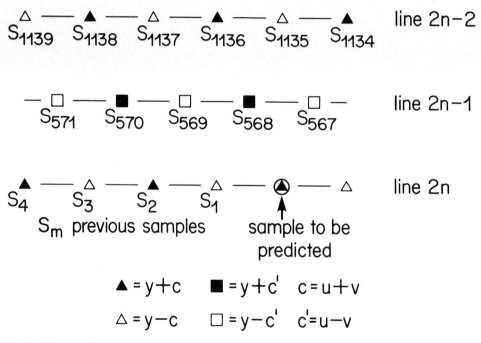

Fig. 7. 2 f_{sc} sampling sites.

Separate Components Digital Video Recording is Needed and Possible

Dominique J. Nasse
CCETT
Rennes, France

The interest and the feasibility of a digital videotape recorder (DVTR) have already been widely discussed and even demonstrated [1,2]. It is generally agreed that the availability of a practical DVTR is the key point that would make fully digital processing of television pictures a reality. This means that a DVTR should not only satisfy the quality, cost, and operational requirements but also operate with a satisfactory digital standard. The first list of requirements is more or less common to all potential users, although some differences appear in the relative weighting of quality vs. investment and operatioanl costs, for example, between the European and U.S. points of view. But the question of the adequate digitizing standards, which for the 525 NTSC system is mainly a matter of choosing a sampling frequency, happens to be more complicated and should be considered in more detail for 625 systems.

The 625/50 color television systems are either PAL or SECAM. Many of the industrially developed countries of the western 50 Hz world are using PAL, and therefore the major part of the research on 625/50 digital television is run by PAL countries, since there is only one SECAM country in Western Europe. However, non-committed observers should not conclude that only PAL is worth considering, since the overall international market is more evenly shared (table 1). Many countries in Africa, Asia, and Eastern Europe are already operating SECAM color television, and have extremely important present and potential needs, though no research on digital television. Some are already asking for all digital plants.

More attention has up to now been paid to the PAL aspect of digital television and therefore of digital recording for 625/50 television. The purpose of this paper is to deal with the specific requirements of digital recording in a SECAM environment and to show how they can be coped with by using picture components.

NECESSITY OF PICTURE COMPONENTS.

The SECAM Signal.

Specifications of the SECAM signal are international standardized [3] and only the main features will be recalled here. The SECAM signal is a frequency domain multiplex of luminance and color information, but unlike PAL and NTSC it uses a frequency modulated subcarrier. This subcarrier can transmit only one signal at a time, and therefore is modulated by R-Y and B-Y baseband signals on alternate lines : the color channel is line-sequential. In the demodulator, a chroma one-line delay permits two frequency discriminators to be permanently fed with chroma (through a line-rate toggle switch) and deliver R-Y and B-Y signals to a matrix. Advantages and disadvantages of the system were widely discussed in the early days of color television in Europe ; since its main feature is to be insensitive to static phase errors, it provides good off-the-air reception (with theoretically no drift in hue and saturation) and easy VTR playback (not requiring color phase processing, full-bandwidth SECAM machines being equivalent to monochrome). The main drawbacks are rather linked to the professional processing.

Mixing.

Since the chroma is frequency-modulated by the baseband information, straight mixing of two composite SECAM signals is not possible. Each of them must be first demodulated into one luminance and one line-sequential baseband color signal ; the two pictures can then have their luminance and color separately mixed. The resulting baseband color signal is remodulated into a chroma which is added to the luminance to give the output composite SECAM (fig.1). Of course, if a fade is performed, limit switches bypass the demod-remod path when the fade is completed with only one picture being involved.

The need for a demod-remod process every time some mixing is required clearly results in the fact that digitizing composite SECAM is of little interest : even though a digital SECAM encoder and decoder can be thought of, the process will remain somewhat complicated and mainly cannot be made transparent. Since the SECAM signal does not provide line frequency interleaving of luminance and chrominance spectra, as it is the case in NTSC and PAL, strong rejection of the subcarrier on the luminance signal must be achieved prior to re-encoding, thereby causing impairements if many passes are involved.

Recording.

As has been pointed out above, the SECAM signal is inherently ruggedized and the VTR playback is relatively simple. When multiple generations are achieved, static phase errors and differential gain effects result in no noticeable impairement. However, noise, linear and non-linear distorsions do build up, limiting the number of generations that can be tolerated in practice.

Digitizing the composite SECAM signal would seem to solve the multiple generations problem, but would in fact forbid the use of a mixer within the loop, which would delete the transparency of the digital path. Obviously, the advantages of such a digital system would not be sufficient to justify new equipments and standards.

The solution is to give up the frequency domain multiplex used by the composite signal and to switch to separate picture components, which in practice will be dealt with in digital as a time-domain multiplex (fig.2). Such a multiplex can be easily mixed and handled without any picture degradation. Picture components are anyway expected to be the normal way of handling television pictures within the production plants in the future, whatever the composite color system.

STANDARDS AND RATES.

Requirements of digital picture components.

It is quite likely that if television was to be completely rebuilt, many features would be designed in a different and better way and many parameters would be unified throughout the world. However, although television systems are different, then do have many features and parameters in common. For example, they all make use of 2:1 interleaved scanning, and basically have the same color space organization ; all 625/50 systems have the same scanning parameters. This results in the fact that many industrial products can be sold to any customer with only minor changes. It is very desirable that in this respect new digital standards should not widen existing gaps and if possible should reduce them. Concerning 625/50 digital picture components, this means that some compatibility must be achieved with composite PAL : a television program should be transcoded from one standard to the other as easily as possible, and equipments should feature as little difference as possible between the corresponding versions.

Work has been carried out within the European Broadcasting Union (EBU, working party C) which is in charge with the standards for the exchange of programs throughout Western Europe. It has already been decided that digital links would carry picture components. Simple compatibility requires the sampling parameters of these components to be simply related to the PAL subcarrier frequency, i.e. the sampling frequencies be integer multiples or sub-multiples of the PAL subcarrier frequency.

Furthermore, another requirement is the level of picture quality : the digitizing parameters should be sufficient to preserve the "studio grade". Besides, the encoding process should be kept simple.

A compatible 625/50 components system.

Weighting these requirements has already resulted in the specification of a compromise [4] whose main parameters will be briefly explained and justified. The picture consists of one luminance Y sampled at approximately 2 Fsc(PAL) and two simultaneous color differences (R-Y an B-Y) sampled at half the luminance sampling frequency, both samples being spatially coincident with one another and with a luminance sample (fig.4).All samples are encoded as 8 bit words. The number of Y samples (462 per active line) is the same as in 2 Fsc PAL, but the line-interleaved pattern repeats every picture, resulting in a "stabilized quincunx" (fig.3). This is why the Y sampling frequency is not exactly 2xFsc PAL, which would yield a moving pattern. This stabilized quincunx structure has been found to be the best compromise when a relatively low sampling frequency (8,87 MHz) is used.

On the other hand, the sampling frequency of the color differences (fsc, 4,43 MHz) is fairly high, and using half that value had been considered ; however, proper color rendition for a good quality picture forbids sharp low-pass fittering of the color differences which causes unacceptable filtering on the color transitions. The 3 dB bandwidth can only be about one half the Nyquist bandwidth, and although the 1/2 Fsc (2,22 MHz)sampling rate is still being considered for transmission purposes, it was not found sufficient for studio picture processing.

The last choice that can be discussed is the interest of two simultaneous color informations. The only drawback is the increased bit rate,which will be discussed later for recording, but is anyway likely to be reduced for transmission purposes. On the other side however, simultaneous color informations remove the problems of horizontal color transitions that can be seen on both picture-stabilized (1-picture cycle, with a phase reversal every picture) and non-stabilized (2-picture cycle i.e. 12.5 Hz, such as SECAM) sequential color schemes. Keying signals can be derived from the picture.

Furthermore, apart from simplifying editing problems and frame stores by making all pictures alike, the selected method has advantages for error protection, which will be dealt with later. Owing to the selected sampling frequencies, the system is usually referred to as "2+1+1", to express its relationship with the PAL subcarrier frequency.

Compatibility and bit rates.

A preferred sampling rate for composite PAL in Europe is 4 Fsc [5]. This results in a picture-lock sampling structure which is nearly perfectly orthogonal, since owing to the 25 Hz offset of the PAL subcarrier (a phenomenon that has no equivalent in NTSC) the samples are not absolutely vertically aligned, but the tilt is so slight (a fraction of a degree) that it can be neglected (fig.5). The quincunx samples can then become part of the 4 Fsc sampling structure, which makes transcoding possible. Further details on the processing involved by bidirectional transcoding do not fall within the scope of this paper. The following results should be emphasized :

-Both 4 Fsc PAL an "2+1+1" have the same overall bit rate of 142 Mb/s prior to any processing ;

-This rate can be restricted to 115 Mb/s at little extra cost by merely eliminating the H blankings, requiring only at least 12 μs of storage (1680 bits). It will be seen that buffering will anyway be required by the error protection system ;

-The quantizing accuracy is comparable to that obtained by 9 bit encoding of composite PAL ;

- The "2+1+1" word stream can be mixed, switched, serialized, transmitted, by the same equipments as 4 Fsc PAL, providing a very desirable "industrial compatibility".

DIGITAL VTR DESIGN AND OPTIMIZATION.

Bit rates.

It is unnecessary to emphasize here the fact that the bit rate and the associated tape consumption is one of the biggest problems of a DVTR. It can be reduced by applying bit rate reduction coding schemes, but also by removing blankings from the recorded information. As has been mentioned earlier the horizontal blanking takes 18% of the time, and at the price of a 25-line buffer advantage could be taken of the vertical interval, with an extra 8% gain, with however some operational drawbacks.

Bit-rate reduction is generally regarded as being useless to magnetic recording because of its complexity and its poor performance in the presence of dropouts. Before discussing the latter, it should be noted that if for example transform coding and variable length encoding result in bulky circuitry, differential coding (DPCM) can be very simple. As mentioned earlier, the color differences are relatively wasteful, and a substantial reduction can be performed while maintaining good quality. Assuming that a 2:1 reduction is achieved, the overall useful rate drops to 86.6 Mb/s with only the H blankings removed (table 2).

Effects of errors.

If any new standard can only be justified by bringing a substantial improvement on existing ones, a digital VTR must completely remove the loss of quality through multiple generations that happens with existing machines. This implies that the effect of errors is still undetectable after a specified (and high) number of generations, say a few tens.

Errors can be coped with by means of two independant methods : correction and concealment. Correction is theoretically more satisfactory, since repeated operation does not result in impairment. However, its efficiency cannot be made perfect, and the residual uncorrected error rate however small will increase linearly with the number of generations. What is worse, the correcting capability is necessary finite and if it happens to be exceeded, the system will sharply stop correcting the errors (and possibly add new ones), thereby causing a severe degradation of the picture. Although errors on magnetic recording may occur in bursts whose length may extend from a few bits to hundreds and even thousands of bits, it is possible to design burst error correcting codes with such correcting capabilies [6], provided that the average error rate is sufficiently low to preserve wide enough error-free areas. But the corresponding circuitry would be rather expensive and bulky, and furthermore its finite capability would not remove the need for a concealment system.

Concealment consists in replacing a section of information impaired by errors by information interpolated from error-free correlated areas. It only requires an error detecting system ; it is not so efficient as correction since some impairment is introduced every time, but it is much safer, since concealment can be performed even mistakenly without catastrophic effects. Good efficiency requires : powerful error detection (with very low probability of non-detection), small size of the replaced area, availability of closely correlated error-free information.

Bit rate reduction systems generally deal with blocks of information separated by "reset" commands. If a block of information contains errors, and if these errors cannot be corrected, the error extension phenomenon impairs the whole block which must be replaced. This generally will not be satisfactory because the bit rate reduction system usually has already used the correlation between adjacent picture elements. It should be noted that the larger the block, the higher the proportion of interpolated information for a given error rate. On the other hand, PCM signals enable pixel per pixel concealment. Furthermore, it is possible to shuffle the information so that words relative to adjacent pixels should not be adjacent on the tape [2] : even in the occurence of a long dropout, every concealed pixel will be surrounded by error-free information, thereby greatly improving the concealment, at the price of some buffering.

Luminance and color differences.

Error concealment has been common practice for a long time in VTR dropout compensators. Errors are detected by a dropout sensor, and the damaged section is replaced by the corresponding section of the previous line, taking advantage of the correlation. Owing to the line-sequential nature of the chroma in 625-line systems, both PAL and SECAM, only the luminance is borrowed from the previous line and the chroma is derived from two lines above. The system still works because the color information is still correlated well enough, while the luminance would not. Furthermore, in SECAM it is not possible to switch chroma within a line since it is frequency modulated, and the whole line of chroma is borrowed from two lines above, with satisfactory results.

This suggests what investigations have now shown : that the visibility of concealment differs widely between luminance and color differences. Color information is quite tolerant and complete television lines can be merely replaced by the previous line many times in every field, or even two lines at a time with a lower rate. Luminance on the other hand seems to be more sensitive by several orders of magnitude. Replacement of a complete line by the previous one is generally noticeable and should be regarded only as a back-up of more efficient methods using shuffling. This justifies the consideration of a 2:1 reduction of the bit rate of the color information and straight PCM for the luminance (table 2), together with the advantages of two simultaneaous color differences. If, for example, DPCM is used, with a simple previous sample prediction, every line containing errors must be replaced, but this will remain invisible. Furthermore, since the active line is more than 1800 bits(color),error detection with extremely low failure probability can be achieved with negligible redundancy [6].

System optimization.

Owing to the requirement of careful error concealment of the luminance information, a most important choice is the error detection system. Whatever the method, the information is split into blocks, and a compromise has to be found, large blocks yielding lower redundancy but increasing the rate of concealment and the resulting impairment [7]. The following method can be used. First assign the rate of concealment that can be tolerated on the final picture (threshold of visibility), then divide by the number of generations that must be guaranteed, which gives the performance of one single record-play process. Assume or measure error statistics. Determine adequate organization resulting in satisfactory concealment rate (by varying methods and block size). Assess required probability of non-detection. Calculate redundancy. Then check for overall bit rate feasibility. If no compromise seems to appear, the use of a correcting system could be considered. This could be of interest if statistics show a high rate of very small bursts or isolated errors. The redundancy will necessarily increase, but it can be minimized by adequately selected strategies.

CONCLUSIONS.

The above methods have been applied to the "2+1+1" 625-line digital components and tend to conclude that a satisfactory arrangement can be found with an overall bit rate of 100 Mb/s approwimately, including redundancy. However high this figure may look, it is not higher than what would be required by composite SECAM and the use of components not only gives the system a far superior quality but also provides the operational flexibility that is mandatory for a digital system. The key point is the error behaviour that can be expected with this bit rate, which greatly depends on the recording format and is best mastered by manufacturers. However it is proven that the extra trouble that is brought by separate color information can be substantially reduced without penalties in error protection. The remaining uncertainty is on the luminance bit rate (i.e. density) and error rate compromise, just as composite signal recording, with some extra advantages in error protection. Since recording is the only remaining bottleneck that prevents interconnection of digital centers, owing to the dropping prices of digital processing electronics, it is believed that the use of components should be considered not only for present or potential SECAM customers, but also when attempting to define a unified or at least compatible digital recording standard.

REFERENCES.

[1] J. Diermann. Digital videotape recording : an analysis of choices, SMPTE Journal vol.87 n°6, June 1978.

[2] J.L.E Baldwin. Recording PAL signals in digital form, Proc.IEE, Vol 125 n°6, June 1978, pp.606-610.

[3] CCIR (Geneva 1974) Report 624, System L.

[4] J. Sabatier, F. Kretz. Sampling the components of 625-line television signals, EBU review, n° 171, october 1978.

[5] Contribution of the EBU to CCIR/CMTT, 11/374 (CMTT 247), 1977.

[6] W.W Peterson and E.J Weldon Jr. Error correcting codes, MIT Press, 1972.

[7] S. Harari, D. Nasse. Protection contre les erreurs en enregistrement magnétique numérique de télévision (error-protection for magnetic digital TV recording), to be published in Annales des Télécommunications, 1979.

Table I. Color television throughout the world.

"SECAM countries" :

Afars & Issas	Iraq
Arab Republic of Egypt	Lebanon
Bulgaria	Luxembourg
Czechoslovakia	Mauritius
France	Monaco
People's Republic of Germany	Poland
Haiti	Saudi Arabia
Hungary	Tunisia
Iran	USSR
Ivory Coast	Zaire

NTSC : 25 countries

PAL   : 36 countries

Mono : 48 countries

No TV : 17 countries

(Source : documents of the
1977 Montreux Symposium)

Table II. Bit rates for 625-line color television.

		Bit rate (MB/s)
(1)	Full "2+1+1" with 3 simultaneous components : one luminance sampled at 8,87 MHz ($\sim$ 2 fsc) Two color differences sampled at 4,43 MHz (fsc)	142
(2)	Same as (1), with color differences reduced to 4-bit words	106
(3)	Same as (2), with H-blankings removed	86,6
(4)	Same as (2), with H and V blankings removed	79,7
(5)	4 fsc PAL	142
(6)	2 fsc PAL	70,9
(7)	Same as (6), with H-blankings removed	$\sim$ 58

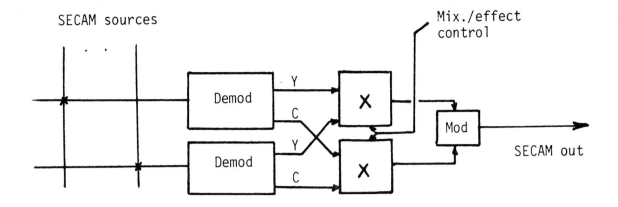

C is line-sequential R-Y/B-Y

Fig. 1. Principle of a SECAM mixer.

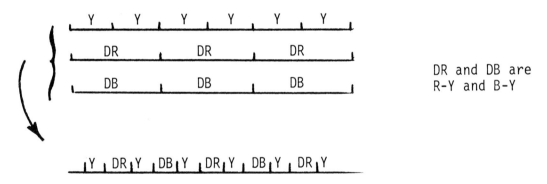

DR and DB are
R-Y and B-Y

Fig. 2. Multiplexing three simultaneous components into a single word stream.

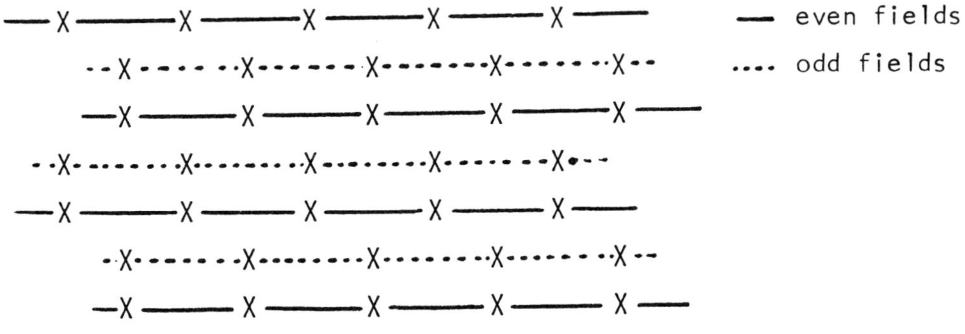

— even fields
.... odd fields

Fig. 3. Stabilized line quincunx sampling structure.

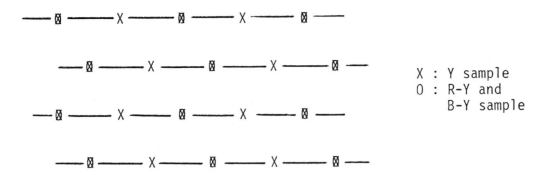

X : Y sample
O : R-Y and
    B-Y sample

(other field identical but shifted downward)

Fig. 4. Sampling patterns of Y, R-Y and B-Y signals.

```
A B C D E F          U V W X Y Z
A B C D E F          U V W X Y Z      Top of raster
A B C D E F          U V W X Y Z

            picture area

A B C D E F          U V W X Y Z
A B C D E F          U V W X Y Z      Bottom of raster
A B C D E F          U V W X Y Z
```

AB..YZ represent the 1135 samples per line
(922 within the picture area)

Fig. 5. 4F$_{sc}$ (PAL) sampling pattern, showing tilt of near-vertically aligned samples.

Dominique J. Nasse began his technical career in 1970 when he joined the research department of the Office de Radiodiffusion Television Francaise (ORTF), which is the French state-owned radio and television network. He was active there in the development of quadruplex and helical VTRs and automated editing systems. Since 1975, he has been with the Centre Commun d'Etudes de Television et de Telecommunications (CCRTT) where he presently leads several research teams on studio-oriented digital television and recording projects. He has contributed recommendations for international standardization to the International Electrotechnical Commission (IEC) and the European Broadcasting Union (EBU).

Digital Video Recording – A Progress Report

M. Lemoine and J. Diermann
Ampex Corporation
Redwood City, California

INTRODUCTION

One year ago at the SMPTE Winter Conference in Atlanta, we presented a paper dealing with an analysis of choices in digital video recording. The design objectives for this new recording technology were established against the reference point of the present one-inch analog technology, which is finding wide acceptance in the broadcast industry. The advantages and disadvantages of various digitizing methods and sampling rates, and their significance for the existing television standards of the world, were weighed against one another. Digital recording of sounds and its specific problems were related to digital recording of video. Finally, the three major methods of scanning magnetic tape were analyzed with respect to their usefulness as a vehicle for digital video signals.

At the International Broadcast Conference in London last year John Baldwin of the IBA described and demonstrated an experimental digital recorder. Today I would like to present another reference point by showing what progress Ampex has made in the laboratory to answer some of the technical questions that have been raised earlier.

The focal point of this progress report is the development of an experimental recorder, which has served and continues to serve as a tool to investigate feasibility and to gain a better understanding of how digital video signals must be treated in a magnetic recording channel. The technical approach chosen combines both innovative and practical elements. To some extent, it modifies existing technology to accommodate the different needs of a digital video signal.

The technical credit for this work goes to Mr. Maurice Lemoine, who has co-authored this paper. He is the principal engineer of a group of dedicated workers who have concerned themselves with digital video recording problems for a considerable period of time.

BASIC APPROACH

The most distinct expectation generally placed upon a digital video recorder applies to its video quality. After one generation we demand very high signal transparency. Beyond the first generation we expect picture deterioration to progress slowly enough such that impairment becomes discernible only after many more generations than is commonly accepted in the analog world. A key question facing the engineer asks to what extent tape saving bit rate reduction methods can be compatible with effective error correction or concealment over many generations. In one way or another all bit rate reduction methods imply compromises in signal transmission. We decided not to start the work relying on such a compromise, but to design a recording system that could transmit a full 8-bit PCM signal in both 625 and 525 line standards with a sampling rate of at least $3 \times f_{sc}$, and possibly $4 \times f_{sc}$ (Figure 1). This means a transmission capability of at least 106 Mb/second and 86 Mb/second, respectively for the two line standards. Obviously, such an approach demands sacrifices in tape consumption and present usage is considerably higher than the 10 square inch/second that has become the standard of analog machines. This approach does not meet all the operational/economic goals of digital video recording; rather it provides a performance benchmark at the high end from which attempts can start to find a compromise between lower tape consumption and inferior signal performance. Such compromises may consist of increased packing density on tape with more objectionable error rates which place greater demands on systems for error correction and/or concealment. They may also consist of primary bit saving schemes, such as sub-Nyquist sampling, DPCM, a mixture of both, or others.

It is not clear at this time whether or not such a cost/performance trade-off is desirable or necessary. The price to be paid for lower tape consumption and the resulting weight and storage volume will be a greater dependence on tape quality resulting in a higher price per square inch and on a more complex error correction system.

COMPONENTS VERSUS COMPOSITE

It is assumed that the television plant and studio, at least within the NTSC and PAL countries, will continue to communicate on a composite level for many years even though more and more picture processing equipment may internally depend on the decoding of the video signal. Therefore, the signal system of the experimental video recorder was chosen to be of the composite type. The available data rate would be sufficient, however, to accommodate component schemes in future developments.

In the SECAM countries, plant and studio operations may be forced towards component communications sooner, due to the difficulties of handling SECAM at the studio level. An interesting and powerful 625 digital component system is being proposed by the CCETT in France. It is compatible with video recording even though its bit rate requirements are higher than would be desirable from a recording and tape usage standpoint.

RECORDING FORMAT

Several authors have stated repeatedly that the key to efficient digital video recording is the use of narrow tracks in conjunction with moderate wavelengths. The problem of following a very narrow recorded track, when playing it back, increases with track length. A transverse recorder, with its short tracks, is a particularly suitable vehicle for writing and reading narrow tracks. For this reason, a two-inch quadruplex scanning system was chosen to be the basic experimental vehicle, even though the word "quadruplex", as will be shown, is no longer appropriate. With its two-inch track length, it performs very well down to the narrow track width required, and suits the purposes of our experimental work.

Following the choice of this well-proven scanner vehicle, the question of writing speed had to be answered. The need to accommodate a bit stream of 86 Mb/second in NTSC, or a bandwidth of approximately 43 MHz in a single head-to-tape channel, would have required a doubling of the conventional quad head-to-tape speed to a range of 3000 to 4000 ips. Such an increase was found to be undesirable for a number of reasons: (1) Centrifugal loads of the scanner would quadruple; (2) Energy exchange effects between heads and tape would become much less predictable; (3) The scanner acoustical noise would become objectionable.

The answer to the questions of writing speed lies in the ease with which parallel and serial operations can be cascaded in digital systems. With two parallel heads and recording channels, each channel can carry one-half of the bit rate, i.e., 43 Mb/second, at a writing speed that is not significantly different from existing quadruplex machines. Beyond the reliance upon well-proven scanning principles this dual channel operation presents certain advantages with respect to error concealment and dropout compensation.

In order to accommodate two instead of one recording channel, the scanner is equipped with 8 instead of 4 heads, and thus turns into an "octoplex" system (Figure 2). Two of the 8 heads are actively reading or writing at any given time. During the write cycle, they accept their respective bit streams from a buffer memory, which in turn is fed by the input A/D converter. Before recording, identification signals and error detection bits are added to the signal. The recording code on tape is a Miller^2 type. It is one of several possible codes designed to match the lack of DC and low frequency response of magnetic recording channels.

The recording format on tape has the following parameters:

Track width:	5 mils
Guard band:	2.5 mils
Head-to-tape speed:	1600 ips
Linear tape speed:	15 ips
Linear packing density:	27 Kbit/inch
Number of lines per dual head pass:	16

On playback, the two parallel head/tape channels are recovered, equalized and decoded. Skew errors between the channels and timebase errors are removed with the aid of recorded identification signals. The error detection and masking systems restore the picture in areas where tape dropouts have occurred. Its performance represents a key factor in the overall subjective acceptability of the digital video picture. Single bit errors, as well as dropouts, detected by checking of the parity bit added to each video word, are masked by separate interpolation

of luminance and chrominance samples from TV lines preceding
and following the dropout line (Figure 3).

AUDIO RECORDING

The performance objectives set for multigeneration video
performance of a digital VTR apply equally to audio performance.
Impairment with dubbing must progress slowly enough to be
compatible with the video side. Error correction or concealment
must be effective and able to compete with the performance of
modern professional audio recorders. It has been our conviction
that (a) only a digital audio channel can meet such objectives,
and that (b) the audio channel or channels can make extensive
use of the digital video circuits available in the machine.
This means that the audio sampling rate must be derived from a
common clock with the video sampling rates in both 525 and 625
line standards. A sampling rate of 50K samples/second is
convenient for this purpose. The only objection that has been
raised publicly against a frequency of 50 KHz as a possible
standard relates to the degree of difficulty with which it can
be converted to the European audio transmission frequency of
32K samples/second.

In addition to the digital audio channels using video read-write
circuits, it will be useful to retain one or several lower
quality analog longitudinal tracks for purposes of editing and
cue messages.

Figure 4 shows the way in which digital audio is recorded on
tape along with the video, providing enough space for four
independent audio channels. A space of 200 mils is provided at
the end of each video head swipe. The independent digital
audio channels are each sampled at a rate of 50K/second and at
a resolution of up to 16 bits per sample. These samples are
stored in a memory that can hold them until the respective
video head has reached the audio recording area and can
discharge the memory onto the tape.

Each audio channel data stream is recorded twice to obtain
immunity to dropout. A powerful error detection system is
used to determine the validity of each sample, and correct
errors when they occur.

DEMONSTRATION

With the presentation of this paper at the conference, a
playback demonstration was given with the following sequence
of video signals:

> Color bars
> Gray field
> Red color field
> Transient response
> Multiburst
> Effect of variable record current
> Four still pictures
> Live camera feed
> Color bars

The intent of this demonstration is to give an impression of the video performance of the experimental VTR along with some formal measurements of its performance.

CONCLUSION AND OUTLOOK

The demonstration shows that digital video recording is feasible and that its quality can be outstanding. The approach taken is based on existing two-inch transverse head/tape technology. It makes no claim to have commercial significance in its present form except perhaps in some specific application areas such as post-production. Here the complete elimination of all analog picture degradations and uncertainties may rate higher than the consideration of operating costs.

It is significant, however, that the technical approach to the digital signal system involves no bit rate compromises whatsoever, and therefore implies no compromises with respect to video performance. A useful benchmark has been reached that can govern further effort. This effort must resolve the balance between lower but acceptable performance, more favorable tape consumption and a packing density on tape that can be maintained not only in the laboratory, but in a practical environment.

It must also resolve all open questions with respect to cost, operating features and diagnostic tools. A digital VTR can only compete in the marketplace if we, as manufacturers, continue to look for thorough solutions to our remaining problems.

Maurice Lemoine was born in 1929 in France and was educated at the University of Paris and the Ecole Superieure des Transmissions (France).

Before joining Ampex, Mr. Lemoine was engaged in the development of wideband microwave communication equipment, radar and navigation equipment.

Mr. Lemoine joined Ampex in 1965 as a Senior Electronic Engineer. He has been engaged in the concept, design and development of Ampex recorder products for the past 14 years. Mr. Lemoine currently holds the position of Senior Staff Engineer. For the past eight years, he has been responsible for the advanced product development of digital video equipment including a prototype digital recorder.

Mr. Diermann was born in 1932 in Leipzig, Germany, and received an MSEE degree from the Institute of Technology in Aachen, Germany, in 1956. The following 10 years, he worked as a design engineer on marine radar system at Atlas-Werke, Bremen, Germany, and at Raytheon Company in Boston, Massachusetts, and San Francisco, California.

In 1966, he joined Ampex Corporation, Redwood City, California, where he was involved in data-recording problems by electron beam and magnetic means in various technical and managerial positions.

In 1976, Mr. Diermann was appointed Chief Engineer for the company's Audio-Video Systems Division; and recently, he has been assigned the position of General Manager, Video Systems Group, developing new products employing digital video and computer technology.

SAMPLING RATE	$2 \times f_{SC}$	$3 \times f_{SC}$	$4 \times f_{SC}$
NTSC	7.2	10.7	14.3 Ms/s
	57.6	85.6	114.4 Mb/s
PAL	8.9	13.3	17.7 Ms/s
	70.9	106.3	141.8 Mb/s
SECAM	/	13.3	17.7 Ms/s
		106.3	141.8 Mb/s

Fig. 1. Sampling and bit rates.

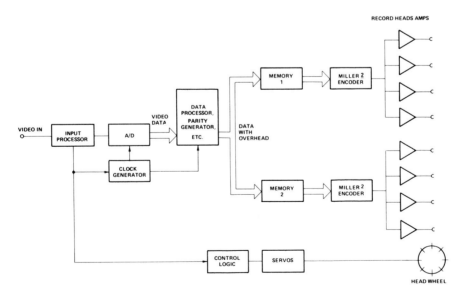

Fig. 2. Digital VTR, record block diagram.

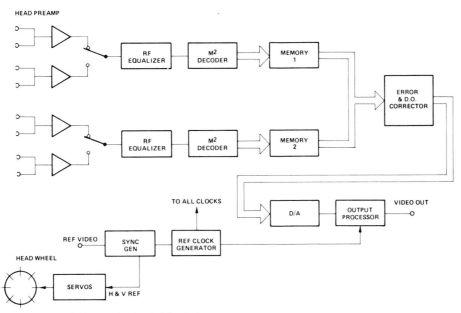

Fig. 3. Digital VTR, playback block diagram.

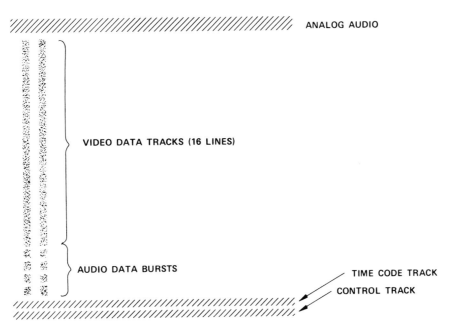

Fig. 4. Digital VTR, tape format.

Digital Video Recording – What Will It Do For The Broadcaster?

Edward H. Herlihy
Golden West Broadcasters
Los Angeles, California

The purpose of this dissertation is to explore what and how broadcasters in the United States think about digital video recording. The paper will examine requirements that broadcasters envision, including features, operating costs, maintainability, interfacing and finally, general observations and views of format and timing of introduction of a viable, digital video recorder.

To properly set the scene, a brief view of what broadcasters know to date about digital video recording seems to be appropriate.

At previous SMPTE Conferences, U.S. manufacturers have given preliminary papers on the technical aspects of digital video recording. These have been theoretical papers giving us a viewpoint from advanced development engineering departments. At the recent International Symposium held on London in September of 1978, two papers were given on digital video recording, as well as a demonstration of digital video recorders, basically designed for the 625 line PAL system.

At this convention, you are aware that AMPEX has demonstrated a laboratory demonstration of a digital video recorder, designed specifically to show capabilities, concepts and advancements in the status of digital video recording. Since this is the first demonstration in the United States of a digital video recorder, most broadcasters have not yet examined its ramifications and benefits.

Briefly summarizing the broadcasters' knowledge, the broadcaster is aware that digital video recording is on the horizon, but in recent surveys taken by the author, the broadcasters are truly unaware of the multitude of problems faced by the manufacturers and their engineers with respect to the design and production of an acceptable digital video recording system. The AMPEX demonstration highlights many of the problems yet to be solved. Perhaps the one major factor that is of concern to all broadcasters is the subject of format or standards for any new digital video recording system.

In the remainder of this report we will try to "crystal ball" information obtained from major broadcasters and manufacturers regarding digital video recording, including the definition of the problems and opportunities in the field.

The typical broadcaster surveyed with respect to digital video recording, expects a major breakthrough, a step forward when a successful digital video recorder is introduced. These expectations are not based on any factual knowledge. It is purely an expectation on the part of the broadcaster that digital video recording will be a "wonder machine". There is a real question whether the digital video recorder will, in fact, be an order of magnitude better than machines in operation to date. Will the DVR be the major step forward that high band was from low band? Will the DVR offer superior signal to noise, as well as all the other capabilities presently offered in production video tape recorders, such as fast picture search, slow motion and reverse action. Information available to date indicates that DVR will be an evolution rather than a revolutionary offering.

There are a lot of problems the broadcasters would like to see digital video recording answer. The following examines them in detail and discusses the salient concepts as viewed by the broadcasters:

1) <u>Standards</u>. Most broadcasters would say in an instant that the effect of another standard in their plant would be a disaster. The realities of the times may prove this is not true once the broadcaster really searches his conscience and examines the problem. For example, the typical broadcaster today probably has in his house, or on order, 2-inch machines, the new 1-inch SMPTE C Format machine, some 3/4-inch U-Matic machines and perhaps a VHS or Betamax 1/2-inch machine. These formats all seem to live within one house compatibly. If one really thinks about it, there is another format in most facilities, the cartridge tape format, even though it uses the standard 2-inch quadruplex format that we all know. Broadcasters must dub to cartridge or cassette. One might as well look at this as another format because there is no direct interchange. Given a few more years, perhaps 5 or a maximum of 7, the broadcasters will probably be willing to readily accept another format, especially a digital format, if it offers them improved performance. We will discuss this topic in more detail later in this paper.

2) <u>Initial Costs</u>. Broadcasters saw almost a 50% capital cost decrease with the advent of presently acceptable 1-inch machines. Given the capabilities of the present 1-inch machines, there is a question whether the broadcasters will accept the higher costs that are estimated for digital video recorders. It has been estimated by several manufacturers that a typical digital video recorder will cost between 125 and 150% of the full cost of a 1-inch machine. This will put the costs somewhere near the middle costs of present quadruplex line of tape recorders. Typically, the broadcasters will spend money for a new piece of equipment if it offers them new features and better specifications. If the foregoing estimates on costs are correct, the manufacturer probably won't have a terribly hard time selling their new hardware.

3) <u>Operating Costs</u>. The broadcasters are increasingly aware of rising operating costs, especially in engineering. The advent of the new 1-inch machines definitely saves operating money, especially in the area of raw stock costs. Knowledgeable broadcasters view the initial thoughts of digital video recording with alarm due to discussions concerning poor packing density for digital video and audio on tape. Basically, the broadcasters' view that the

operating costs can't be any worse than the present 2-inch machines and should be more like 1-inch machines. Obviously, the broadcasters would like to see reduced costs of operation, with respect to the mechanical parts that wear on present machines. The cost of head rebuild on a quadruplex machine is now $1,000 to $1,400. This is an area where cost reduction could be realized.

4) Specifications. Broadcasters basically desire a "transparent" digital video recorder. This is idealistic, but perhaps in the area of realism as we look at the conceptual approach offered by AMPEX at this meeting. The broadcasters are looking for a machine with minimum mechanical errors, lack of dropouts and a signal to noise area of at least 55 and more like 65 db. They desire excellent tape handling capability and the best possible audio capability with 2 to 4 tracks available. The audio portion of the machine should offer absolutely flat response with a minimum of distortion. More attention should be paid to audio in a digital video recorder than has been paid to audio in machines heretofore produced.

5) Machine Features. The broadcasters obviously do not want to give up in a digital video recorder any of the advances they have obtained with machines so far offered on the market. Stop action, slow motion and reverse action are all desirable features, as well as viewable picture at high forward speeds for faster edit decision-making. There are other concepts and features that could be considered in a digital video recorder, including the storing of single frames, the capability of having the machine act as a frame synchronizer and perhaps the capability of slow speed recording for information storage over a long period of time.

6) Maintainability. Digital video recording emphasizes the computer age. The broadcasters are just getting into computers and finding out what computers can do for broadcast engineering. The concept of self diagnosis with respect to any new equipment is certainly a distinct advantage. Any type of computer assist that aids in maintaining the machine, would be viewed with a very positive reaction by the broadcasters.

7) Interfacing. Heretofore, the broadcasters have had a fair degree of difficulty in interfacing video tape recorders with remote control and computer editing systems, the latter being the most difficult. Even present 1-inch machines are difficult to interface with present computer editing systems. Usually the broadcaster is faced with purchasing or constructing "black boxes" to interface his equipment with editing hardware. These areas need to be examined by the manufacturers and simplified or standardized in the future offering.

8) Cartridge/Cassette Formats. As mentioned briefly earlier, we must consider the cartridge/cassette format presently used by the broadcasters as another format. Many broadcasters feel that a digital cassette recorder could be

made smaller and less expensively than the present AMPEX and RCA offerings. This may be a misplaced notion, but there seems to be a desire to see a digital video cassette machine. This is certainly something for the manufacturers to ponder, however, it does not seem realistic to develop a cassette or cartridge machine prior to developing the open reel equipment. This at least expresses the broadcasters' desire to see more work done to update the present cartridge/cassette format.

With all of these views and concepts in mind, the one area that stands out as the broadcasters' biggest concern is standards for a digital video recorder. The broadcasters ask how will standards be developed? Will the broadcasters be involved? If they are, how will they be involved? Will the manufacturers come out with various formats which will cause consternation amongst the American broadcasters and a lack of interchangeability in the business. These questions intimately involve the broadcasters and the manufacturers.

It became obvious from my discussion with major broadcasters, that they want an engineering group such as the SMPTE, to lead the way. This is difficult conceptually from the way standards have been set in the past.

A little history is in order to point out the nature of the standards setting problem that faces digital video recording. In 1957, AMPEX introduced the 2-inch quadruplex format that we know today. Other manufacturers picked up the same format and generally, this was turned into a recommended practice for 2-inch recording. Later, AMPEX introduced the concept of high band recording. The SMPTE was involved in settling concepts between AMPEX and other manufacturers. The SMPTE finally helped to set standards. Super high band pilot-tone standards were proposed by various manufacturers and ultimately settled upon through SMPTE. In the area of 1-inch recorders, several manufacturers showed varying formats of 1-inch machines. The broadcasters became very much involved and put pressure on the manufacturers to develop a standard. This standard was negotiated through the auspices of SMPTE.

Digital video recording must be viewed in a different light. To this date, no viable product has been introduced, nor have there been any discussions amongst the broadcasters or the manufacturers with respect to standards. As we have seen today, there is adequate demonstration that a digital video tape recorder can be constructed. While the AMPEX offering is only a report, it does demonstrate how far we have come. If other manufacturers are to introduce machines, we will have chaos in the industry with respect to digital video recording. Despite the problems of getting manufacturers together prior to product introduction, it seems to be a viable suggestion that the SMPTE undertake immediately to start setting digital video recording standards. To do this will be frought with problems, especially since the manufacturers will be reluctant to discuss in a group their engineering secrets and advancements. It will take some time to set standards. However, it is a strong desire of American broadcasters that standards be set prior to machine introduction. timing is not a real problem, as the best guess is that broadcasters will be willing to accept a new format in 5-7 years.

One further thought. The manufacturers themselves cannot get together to set standards. This violates antitrust laws. Only an independent organization such as the SMPTE can be the viable means to set these kinds of standards. Broadcasters urge that this organization immediately begin formation of a committee and send inquiries to all manufacturers interested in digital video recording to see if interest can be developed to set standards for this new product.

This will be a long and difficult task. It may require some changes in the SMPTE Bylaws, but the end result will be best for all concerned so that digital video recording will arrive as a viable and useful product for the broadcasters.

Edward Herlihy, vice president of engineering for Golden West Broadcasters, is in charge of corporate engineering and acquisitions, labor relations, long-range planning and duties as a FCC liaison.

Herlihy, who became vice president in 1977, brings to his position a strong technical background. Prior to his current assignment, he served as director of engineering for KTLA-TV, director of technical services for Kaiser Broadcasting Company and sales engineer for RCA Broadcast Equipment.

Herlihy graduated from Boston University with a major in communications and served for three years in the U.S. Army Signal Corps.

Digital Video Recording —
A Panel Discussion from the 13th SMPTE Television Conference

SAN FRANCISCO, 3 Feb. 1979

Edit. Note: A mark of the importance of digital technology to the television industry is seen in the fact that the SMPTE has arranged two panel discussions on the subject only three months apart. The first, dealing with the near-term future of digital television, was held during the 120th Conference in New York. The present panel discussion on digital video recording was held on Saturday afternoon, 3 February, following five papers on the same subject. The panel was comprised of the authors of those five papers along with four additional people with digital television expertise. Panelists (and their affiliations) included:

Donald V. West (Moderator), *Broadcasting* magazine;

Peter Rainger, British Broadcasting Corp.;

Charles Ginsburg (Chairman, SMPTE Study Group on Digital Television), Ampex Corp.;

Dominique Nasse, CCETT (a French TV research center);

Joachim Diermann, Ampex Corp.;

Edward Herlihy, Golden West Broadcasters;

K. Blair Benson, Video Corp. of America;

Arch Luther, RCA Corp.;

Marcel Auclair, Canadian Broadcasting Corp.

As is usual, questions and comments were also entertained from the floor. Here is the transcript of the Digital Video Recording panel discussion.

Mr. West: Our purpose this afternoon, the nine of us on the platform and you in the audience, is to try to sum up what has been determined about video, digital video recording over the last few years and what the immediate and long-range futures might be. In addition to the gentlemen who have presented papers this afternoon, we have three additional panelists, Blair Benson, Arch Luther and Marcel Auclair. I am going to ask Mr. Luther to give us his impressions first.

Let me tell you a little about him. He is Chief Engineer of the Commercial Communications Systems Division at RCA. That division embraces four principal areas of operation, broadcast equipment being the main one. He's been with RCA for 28 years. He is here this afternoon to represent the point of view of the equipment manufacturer. Mr. Luther.

Mr. Luther: I would like to take up briefly the issue of the objectives for digital recording in terms of system cost and system performance. One requirement for any new recording system to be accepted in the marketplace is that the system must have the proper relationship to existing systems in terms of both cost and performance parameters.

Nevertheless, the marketplace needs a *range* of these parameters, from low-cost systems that fulfill moderate performance requirements to high-cost systems which meet the most sophisticated performance needs that any of us can imagine. Where does digital recording fit into this cost and performance range? And what goals should we as digital designers strive for?

I think these questions can be approached by first comparing some of these fundamental characteristics of digital and analog recording to understand which areas of the cost/performance arena are best addressed by digital technology? Without spending a lot of time on this, I come to the conclusion I think most people here today also do: that digital recording can achieve higher performance levels that analog and this has been demonstrated. On the other hand, digital recording requires smaller wavelengths and smaller tracks on the tape to really be economical, and this demands greater mechanical sophistication and electronic servo and correction systems.

Furthermore, we can expect that digital recording will be initially more complex and more costly than present high-performance analog recorders. Therefore, it seems clear that digital recording is best suited to address the market at the high-performance, high-cost end.

To do that successfully, I would recommend that digital system designers seek to improve the performance parameters most often criticized in analog recording and that they put these improvements ahead of cost considerations. Some of the likely areas are signal-to-noise ratio, multigeneration capability, video bandwidth and, very importantly, performance of sound channels. We should not let cost considerations cause us to compromise these issues. I would even make cost tradeoffs to achieve the performance objectives — for example, the use of four-times-subcarrier video sampling, rather than three-times. Or the use of full error correction rather than concealment. Or many other areas where you can improve performance if you accept the costs.

This approach of putting the emphasis on high performance allows the development of a digital recording system which will have initial applications which are not now being reached by analog recording. Later, as further development allows the cost of digital recording to be reduced, it will be possible to address other market segments and broaden the application of the system.

The standards for the systems should remain the same, however, so that a single standard would have the broadest long-term application. This would not be achieved if we make performance tradeoffs in the interest of early product introductions or initial low costs.

Mr. West: Our next speaker is Blair Benson who is Vice-President for Engineering and Technical Operations for the Video Corporation of America. He appears here this afternoon also representing the Video Tape Producers' Association, and essentially his is the point of view of the production house. Before joining VCA in 1976, Blair was Vice-President for Engineering of Goldmark Communications Corp., and before that — from 1945 to 1972 — he was with CBS as Director of Audio-Visual Engineering. Mr. Benson.

Mr. Benson: Since I think the major benefit from a panel discussion of this sort is an exchange between the audience and the panelists, my remarks will be necessarily short. As we have said, my role is to represent the viewpoint of the production house. It is the production house that makes both commercials and a variety of program materials, not only for broadcasting but also for educational purposes and for industrial use.

I might note that digital video is not in itself new to the production houses. We are already well versed in the use of the digital noise reducer, for example, and it is gaining widespread use. We are going to see an increase in the use of digital video this year in the form of framestore processing equipment, such as the Grass Valley, Quantel and Vital framestores. These are going to add a new dimension to electronic post production.

Going beyond existing equipment, we have a vital interest in the future of digital video recording, particularly in avoiding the need for decoding and coding – going back and forth between the various black boxes and the digital video recorders and playback equipment. A year or two ago it seemed that multiple codecs in tandem would produce levels of degradation that might be unacceptable. Now, however, we are encouraged by Charlie Ginsburg's report that the degradation today is minimal. This finding opens up a whole new vista for this particular system design.

Furthermore, in regard to digital recording, I think it is essential that we have a system which has such a low noise level that multiple generations of recording and reproduction become possible – at least five to seven and possibly eight or even ten generations, in order to provide a maximum of flexibility in post-production work. This is imperative if we are going to compete with what has been done in the past with film optics and film animation in the film labs. Based on the papers we have just seen on computer animation, it seems that computer animation *will* compete with film animation – but again this is tied in to digital recording and digital processing.

All this talk about digital recording is coming at a paradoxical time however. Two years or more ago, before the advent of the current one-inch helical equipment, I would have said, "This is something we must have. Let's rush the development. Let's get it to the marketplace. The problems with quad (high maintenance, high head cost, difficulty in maintaining quality in the face of banding and head separation and one-line error and so on) have been just monumental and expensive to cope with."

Now, two years have passed and the situation is different. I think we have reached a level of development with the one-inch equipment that makes the production house look at the digital approach with a jaundiced eye. Do we really need it? Can we afford it? The operating and capital costs for one-inch equipment are already coming down and the quality is up. It's solving a lot of the problems we had with quad, so unless digital video offers us some order-of-magnitude improvements in performance and some drastic reductions in costs, I don't see a great demand for it in the immediate future.

Mr. West: Our final panelist from whom we are asking comments is Marcel Auclair, Assistant Director of the Studio Systems Department at Engineering Headquarters of the Canadian Broadcasting Corp. in Montreal. He has been with CBC for 15 years in a variety of engineering posts and is on the panel to represent the view of a major broadcasting user. Mr. Auclair.

Mr. Auclair: It is my opinion that digital video recording is definitely the way to go. Still I would think that broadcasters in general are faced with the same problem we have had in the CBC – the lack of experience in maintaining digital equipment. We first encountered this problem in connection with the time-base corrector: we found that although the technology was quite perfect, we did not have sufficient technical maturity in general across the network to properly maintain this equipment.

So, before any organization really contemplates using digital technology, I think they should consider that there will be a major impact not so much on the operating staff but on the maintenance staff, to properly maintain and debug that equipment. Nevertheless, neither these difficulties nor any needs to achieve standardization should be allowed to forestall the development of any useful equipment – from a very highly portable piece of gear to a very, very complex machine that should be used only in the studio.

We have already seen such problems: standardization and the one-inch format; how to get quad to go portable, etc. The more broadcast grows, the more we want the flexibility to go outside. (I'm not referring here to ENG: I am referring to on-site shooting, using isolated cameras.) The broadcaster wants a very highly portable recorder, and if a desire for standardization gets in the way of the designer trying to come up with something small, that would be where we throw away the ball game.

Whatever other consequences the digital video recorder would bring for studios, we would anticipate that there would be a significant reduction of capital costs. If this doesn't happen, the digital VTR would not be very appealing to us. The other cost that should also be contemplated is the *operating* cost, and that also should be reduced appreciably relative to quad or one inch.

The necessity for set-up controls should be reduced as much as possible. Intelligent diagnostic systems ought to be part of the system to facilitate maintenance and debugging. It goes without saying that the digital VTR must be highly reliable. We agree with the view that we broadcasters should be more involved in the design or the proposed design of new equipment. We know the tools that we want, and we are in the field. It will be best for all of us if manufacturers come and consult with us first.

Mr. West: Now, we will invite questions and comments from the audience. We are very fortunate, it seems to me, to have assembled here people with so much information about digital tape recording. I would say that virtually everything known is known here. Do we have a question?

Emil Kratochvil, KTLA, Hollywood: I would like to comment first that I was quite impressed with the demonstration of the codec (coder/decoder) system evaluation tape. My question is: Has any attention been given to intermixing codecs of different manufacturers using different sample rates? Since the same model of codec was used in the demonstration, I assume they all used the same sampling rate. I would like to know if degradation of a signal has been studied, using different sample rates and intermixing them. If not, I should think that another demonstration would be in order.

Mr. Ginsburg: I will be very glad if some company chooses to undertake such an experimental program. It is a very big task and difficult to do. As far as I know, no experiments have been made to determine how the impairments vary as codecs employing different sampling rates are used. I would expect, however, that the three-times sampling rate which we used would be the worst case.

Mr. Kratochvil: You feel that would be worse than intermixing them? As we broadcasters use a signal, we don't necessarily know how many or which types of codecs it has been through. Then, we pass the signal through a codec having a sampling rate that could be different from that of the codecs it previously passed through, possibly degrading the signal.

Mr. Ginsburg: It seems to me that an agency that could properly be identified as completely objective would have to conduct such tests. Otherwise the hues and cries about parochialism in finding more faults with one manufacturer's equipment than another's would be deafening.

Al Goldberg, CBS Technology Center: I will direct this question to Mr. Ginsburg, in his capacity as chairman of the SMPTE Digital TV Study Group. The matter of whether the television plant will eventually become all-digital has been examined by your committee. It was pointed out that the lack of a digital VTR is a stumbling block, because – after all – why use an analog VTR in an all-digital plant? Therefore, would I be correct in assuming that if a digital VTR becomes available it will be a significant step forward toward the ultimate digital television plant? How do you see that as a factor in the design of the digital VTR?

Mr. Ginsburg: Well, digital videotape recording certainly appears to be

ENG/EFP in one hand...

...studio/field production in the other

from VICTOR DUNCAN *VIDEO*

MNC-71CP

offers the latest state-of-the-art prism optics and the reliability of LSI circuitry. A light, fast, on-the-shoulder video production camera for news and fast moving field production assignments.

MNC-710CP

for studio/field production, the MNC-710CP affords all the quality features of the MNC-71CP, plus a camera mounted 5″ viewing monitor, remote production control unit, "paint box" and rack-mounted teleproduction CCU. In this studio/field production format, the MNC-710CP is a high quality color production camera that meets all NTSC broadcast standards.

For all your video production needs—cameras, recorders, lighting, support and accessories—contact the largest film and video equipment house in the Midwest.

do-able. There are a lot of questions yet to be answered. I think that if someone had the funds to make the installation of an all-digital television plant on an experimental basis, that it could be done at this time. Unfortunately nobody seems to have the money to do it.

Mr. Benson: I'd like to add one comment. Regarding the all-digital plant, I can't foresee that as coming in the immediate future any more than I can the digital videotape machine. I do feel, however, that we are going to see new television plants which will employ fiber optics. In so doing, they will get away from all of this complexity of coaxial cables and connectors and what have you. I think that that aspect of digital is definitely the wave of the future.

Mr. Diermann: I would like to compare these advances to the development of the telephone system, where you still have crank telephones working out at the boondocks with international satellite connections. The studio isn't going to go digital from one day to the next. It's going to be an evolutionary process during which new equipment will need to interface on an analog basis for a long period of time and still have a digital port to be ready to go digital when its neighbors do. More and more of interconnections will be digitized by degrees, but, for both technical and economic reasons, the conversion won't happen all at once.

Joe Roizen, Telegen: All of the digital VTRs that have been so far demonstrated have involved segmented scanning. The IVC 9000 was used for the first IBA experiments and the BCN for the next set and then the Ampex quad for the next. We are now entering a period of rapid growth of one-inch helical Type-C machines which use a single head for field scanning. Are we going to see those machines disappear when the digital VTR comes along, or are people going to figure out how to make the helical machines work digitally and provide a handy dandy conversion kit for the customer?

Mr. Diermann: It seems to me that in digital VTR the question of how many segments you have for each television field or frame is no longer really meaningful — not as far as basic picture performance is concerned. You are dealing with a bit bucket. You might look on the digital VTR as taking a digital time-base corrector and placing the VTR right in the center. It isn't quite that simple, but that's the general principle. So segmentation does not create any of the conventional errors in a digital system.

Segmentation or the way you organize the recording on tape, of course, does relate in some way to the manner in which you might want to accomplish special effects (such as still frame, slow motion, the ability to see a picture at high tape speeds), so there it may play a role, for mechanical reasons or logistic reasons.

Now as to the second portion of your question: do you expect to see retrofit kits for existing formats? I really don't.

Robert Liftin, Regent Sound Studios: I would like to address this question to the panel. Right now in the audio field, we have a fiasco with three or four different digital standards for audio recording. In the video field, although Ampex does have a digital format, their machine was today demonstrated without the audio. The AES currently has a committee that is lumbering along deciding on a digital format for audio. I wonder whether the panel feels that the SMPTE should get involved in some way in terms of the standards for digital audio and somehow try to marry this together, as opposed to letting the whole issue be free-wheeling.

Mr. Benson: Digital audio standardization is a hot potato at the moment. The SMPTE has had meetings and discussions with the AES, as to who should handle it. I will just mention that there is a Justice Department problem here which has to be solved first, and it appears that the Japanese may jump the gun and develop and agree upon standards in Japan before any action can be taken here in the U.S. because of our legal problems. The AES is now going ahead with the committee to study this but how fast they will respond and come up with something remains to be seen. In the meantime, both 3M and Sony have digital systems which are going to be used. The Sony system, I think, is already being embraced by at least three major recording studios for making their masters. It works quite well and has excellent characteristics. Thus, there will be some use of digital audio in the U.S. in advance of standardization.

Mr. Herlihy: I think that the audio fiasco just mentioned could be a prelude for a horrible video fiasco. That's the thing that a lot of broadcasters are really concerned about — the proliferation of various digital video recorders into the marketplace, perhaps too soon. We could be faced with the same thing that the audio people are faced with right now. I don't think that it's going to be easy at all to get the manufacturers into one room and standardizing. I gather it was pretty difficult getting agreement on the Type-C format, and you can imagine what it will be like when none of them have really introduced anything. So it will be difficult, and it will be time

consuming. I think, however, that we *do* have time to anticipate this problem and deal with it. Now, everybody is excited about the one-inch machines; they are buying them in droves. The price is pretty good, the quality is excellent, the features are things we have long waited for, and we are all rushing around, madly stocking up. So Blair Benson's question was a good one: "Do we need digital machines right now?" For the help it may be: some tape manufacturers claim there is a turnover cycle of five to seven years for videotape formats. They have seen this in the United States ever since videotape recording started. So, I think we have got the time to get ready. In five to seven years, or maybe ten years, we can expect to be dealing with digital video recording formats.

Mr. Auclair: Would it not be appropriate for the SMPTE to begin studying the matter of digital recording, with no commercial orientation other than for broadcasters to state what they want? How the box works on the inside is totally immaterial. What *we* want, for example, is a portable box of tricks that weighs ten pounds and can record for a given length of time. In a studio in Timbuktu, they may also need a simple recorder just to play a program. Someone else wants to have all kinds of effects — to edit and post-edit. Wouldn't now be the right time to assemble a group of broadcasters and write some kind of a white paper around digital VTRs and digital audio recorders?

Roland Zavada, Engineering Vice-President of SMPTE: Yes, it is possible for broadcasters to provide input. The Society is structured to study engineering problems by our concept of study groups whose purpose is to derive technical data on an informational basis, that could be used to develop documents that might result as standards or recommended practices. I could speak with you afterwards, and we *could* make an invitation to users, broadcasters and any others that wish to review this problem from a study standpoint. We must be careful about this for several reasons. First, as Blair has noted, the Justice Department has been involved and concerned on some of the aspects of standardization prior to commercial introduction. (You will recognize that the Society's policy has been generally to *document* practice, not to *invent* practice.) The second reason is that we are also faced now with a significant Federal Trade Commission proposed rule-making in the entire field of standards certification and implementation, and the Society is addressing these problems through its legal counsel. That, however, doesn't preclude study of the

It's in the cards.

The solution to your next switching problem is probably built into one of our new System 21 cards.

We've unsnarled many a complicated distribution switching puzzle during our 22 years in the audio, video and data switching business. So, when we developed this new state-of-the-art system, we created an architecture that would let us move with cost-effective ease from 10 x 10 to 1000 x 1000 inputs and outputs.

What's your requirement? Our standard video cards in television broadcast applications offer specification numbers like 0.15% differential gain, 0.15° differential phase and ±0.1-dB frequency response to 5 MHz. Other video cards operate at 30-MHz bandwidths in high resolution environments.

Audio cards keep harmonic distortion under 0.25% at full 30 dBm output with hum and noise riding 105 dB below. They're balanced in and out and are protected against short circuits for an indefinite period. Worst case crosstalk isolation is greater than 80 dB to 15 kHz.

Cards are instantly replaceable with power on. They're controlled by a microprocessor with battery-backed memory so loss of power doesn't lose the matrix setting.

Controls, a variety of standard configurations, all operate on a single coaxial cable, or you might find our RS-232 port and your computer the best answer.

Yes . . . it's in the cards. We know we can be of assistance to you so call or write for additional information.

DYNAIR ELECTRONICS, INC.
5275 Market Street, San Diego, CA 92114
Tel.: (714) 263-7711 TWX: (910) 335-2040

problem and open dissemination of the derived information for the use of manufacturers and others in trying to develop specifications that could result in the highest possible degree of compatibility.

Mr. West: I would like to get my own question in here for a moment to the panel. As a journalist, I tend to approach these things much more in a "gee whiz" fashion than the engineers who are much more familiar with what is going on. I was really impressed that at 3:45 this afternoon, in this room, we saw the first demonstration by an American manufacturer of digital video recording. And I wonder how impressed other people were by what they saw. I would like to put a question, my first question, to Mr. Luther of RCA: What did RCA think of what Ampex demonstrated today?

Mr. Luther: I'm not going to make an official RCA statement, but my personal observation is that the Ampex machine has demonstrated what we all knew could be done with the approach that they took.

Mr. West: Next, I would like to get additional reactions from the panel and then I would like to hear a comment from the floor also on this point – what you potential users of this system thought. First, I would like to go to our European friends and ask Mr. Rainger and Mr. Nasse what they thought of the Ampex demonstration? Mr. Rainger, please?

Mr. Rainger: I thought that it was a fine achievement, one which I applauded with the rest of you. I think it is an excellent thing to do. You have to overcome hurdles before you get this thing working. There are three hurdles that have been jumped; we have seen stationary head machines, digital video recorders with helical-type rotating heads, and now transverse rotating heads. There are about 30 more hurdles to go before we have a working machine which meets all the requirements that have been listed, but a great deal has been learned and every hurdle cleared is another one out of the way.

Mr. West: Mr. Nasse.

Mr. Nasse: What impressed me in the demonstration was that although the tape consumption was not so low as the IBA machine, it was not tremendously high and the picture quality was very superior.

Mr. West: Questions or observations from the floor? If there aren't any, I would like to go back to one of the gentlemen from Ampex, either Mr. Diermann or Mr. Ginsburg, and ask you to tell us what *you* think of the demonstration this afternoon? If you wonder about my question, I used to have a rule in working with Dr. Frank Stanton at CBS to ask, "Now that it's perfect, what's wrong with it?" Now that you have gotten this perfect, what's wrong with it?

Mr. Diermann: It's, of course, difficult to make a negative statement about something positive. Its operational cost is too high. Its weight and size are too great. It isn't portable, obviously. It doesn't have a number of the features and special effects that we have accepted as perfectly normal in the everyday one-inch environment.

And, without going into detail, there are a number of internal questions that need to be solved. So, I agree with Mr. Rainger that there are at least 30, or possibly 31, problems ahead of us.

Mr. West: This next question is a follow-up to a concern that Ed Herlihy seems to have – that we may face a number of manufacturers flooding the market with various digital VTRs. My own uneducated impression is that there is great reluctance on the part of any manufacturer to go into making digital VTR; and therefore I would ask you, Mr. Ginsburg, "Is it possible that the demonstration that you have given today was designed as much to discourage digital as to encourage it?"

Mr. Ginsburg: Not from *my* standpoint, it wasn't. Of course, you must realize that there is nothing on the market right now. The point of this demonstration today was to make a technological progress report.

Mr. West: One of the impressions that I have gotten from this session and from being in the hall is that there

is almost a 180° difference in approach between the Europeans and the Americans in this field. Is that correct? And would any of you who have seen, as I have not, the IBA demonstration of last year and today's demonstration, comment on how far apart on a spectrum those two approaches are? Mr. Diermann.

Mr. Diermann: Yes, I would like to say something on this subject. I believe John Baldwin and we at Ampex started with totally different premises and at opposite ends of the spectrum. I believe he said to himself, "Let's see how we can make a digital machine with a tape consumption that is comparable to present analog systems (ten square inches or so per second) and let's squeeze a PAL signal system into what is available, no matter what the picture performance." I really cannot personally comment a great deal on the picture performance because no test signals were used in London; he shoots from film and the viewing conditions weren't perfect. That's how John Baldwin, I believe, started: so much tape is

what's allowed and now I squeeze the signal in and I use some bit-rate-reduction method like sub-Nyquist sampling. We, as I showed in the paper, started from the opposite end. We said to ourselves, "Let's not make a compromise as far as the signal system is concerned, and let's, for the time being, to take the first step, not worry about the tape consumption.

Mr. West: Mr. Rainger, if you have a comment on that point.

Mr. Rainger: The demonstration which IBA gave indeed did have an objective similar to that which you have just heard. The compromise, I think, was not very *much* of a compromise, in terms of picture quality, and such impairment as it introduced I have shown today could be removed without much difficulty. The major difference I saw between these two demonstrations is in the visibility of errors. For various reasons, which I am not in a position to explain, there were a lot more errors in the IBA demonstration than I saw here. Whether that is due to error correction or con-

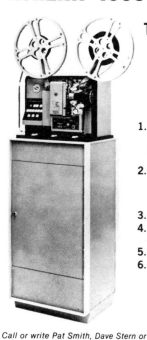

cealment I don't know, but the result here I thought was very good.

Mr. Roizen: I have had the good opportunity, Don, of seeing all of the machines at one time or another and rather close up, except this one. This was my first look at the Ampex machine and I was sitting about 20 feet from a monitor, and I still have 20/30 vision or so. The IBA machine does not work as well as this one. This one is far superior in terms of picture quality and in terms of the amount of error that you can see. There is no question about that. The IBA machine, when I saw it in London at the latest demonstration they gave, had very visible errors. In fact, after they had explained to me what I was looking at, I commented that it reminded me of the old days of Ampex with the early machines, because they had come up with the three things we always would tell people who were coming in to look at the VR1000. The first thing they said was that the picture source was lousy. Secondly, they said that they hadn't picked a good piece of tape. And thirdly, they used the title of my next book: "Don't go by that monitor."

But to get serious for a minute, Ampex has an advantage in the sense that they are using three times subcarrier to start with (a lower subcarrier signal). The pictures we saw in Europe were PAL; these are NTSC. NTSC is obviously somewhat easier in terms of the bandwidth required and so on. The other thing is that the IBA is using an error concealment technique which is a far way from being perfect. (In fact, what Peter Rainger said today about *his* $2F_{sc}$ approach may have a significant effect on what the IBA is doing with *their* $2F_{sc}$. The IBA's machine at the International Broadcasting Convention was not being shown to the general attendance, but I requested to see the machine and was permitted to. While I was there, I asked one of the engineers if he could shut off the error concealment just so I could see what the picture would look like. He did, and the picture showed considerable impairment. It takes a lot of error concealment to make that system work. Perhaps what Peter was talking about may cure that problem. So, in effect, we have seen a very impressive and certainly the best demonstration of digital video recording on moving tape (not disks, not other means) that I think anybody has seen to date, and that certainly speaks well for what Ampex has done.

Mr. West: I think that alone — what you have said about the quality of the Ampex demonstration — makes the afternoon worthwhile.

E. Stanley Busby, Ampex Corp.: A question of Mr. Nasse and Mr. Rainger.

In Europe I know they transmit audio around by a thirteen-bit system on intercity links, and I wonder, "Is the dynamic range that this offers greater or less than the dynamic range maintained by the FM stations in Europe." I have tried to find out what sort of dynamic range FM stations have in Europe and I haven't been able to find out.

Mr. Rainger: That's fairly simple to answer. The distribution system which they have been using for some years is thirteen bits but it's with companding. In other words, the signal is compressed and expanded before it goes through the communication system, and the net result is that the dynamic range of the signal that is being radiated by the FM transmitters is now better than it's ever been before, and people enjoy better quality than they have ever had before. However, it is worth saying that new equipment is being developed for distribution purposes on a two-megabit standard link, and these are all being based on fourteen-bit samples, not thirteen. I think that the change, however, is not made to get a better dynamic range but to improve the signal/noise ratio under certain difficult circumstances.

Patrick Ramsay, BBC, London: Far be it from me to make a value judgment on the IBA demonstration. I am not an engineer, Mr. Chairman, which is perhaps why I have a touching faith in their ability to solve all technical problems. It seems to me that there may be a whole range of problems elsewhere which we have hardly touched on in these two days, although Mr. Oudin did make one reference to them. We are in the middle of a whole range of technical and technological changes. All the problems sooner or later are quite clearly going to be solved. But what about the people who are then going to use the resulting equipment? I would like to ask the panel what they think that the present changes we've been discussing for two days and the increasing rate of change are going to do to employment prospects within the broadcasting industry and to industrial relations within the broadcasting organizations.

Mr. West: May I suggest that Ed Herlihy field that first?

Mr. Herlihy: I had an appropriate discussion along those lines today. I was talking to a gentleman from the American Broadcasting Company who has just made a tour in major markets looking for maintenance engineers (as many of us are prone to do, from time to time; more so lately). In the United States I think it would be safe to say we are already in deep trouble just finding maintenance people. I can speak only from the view of our own plant where we employ some 100

THINKING VIDEO? THINK CAMERA MART.

Because at Camera Mart, we feature an entire line of video equipment including Ikegami, Hitachi, Panasonic, Sony, Microtime and many others. The Ikegami ENG package shown here is just one of many we offer. It's got everything you need to cover the story, indoors or out.

The camera: Ikegami's HL-77, the completely self-contained, high sensitivity Plumbicon®* color shoulder camera that's light weight and easy to handle. Its low-profile, with eye-level CRT monitor (on both take and playback, by the way), gives it the convenience and maneuverability you'll appreciate during those hectic, on-the-spot coverage sessions.

The recorder: Sony's easy-to-operate VO-3800

gives you up to 20 minutes of NTSC color on a single U-Matic® cassette which can be edited on the 2860.

This custom package and *whatever* you need in video, are all available for sale, rent or through convenient lease-purchase options which can be arranged to suit nearly any budget. And we're flexible, too. If there's a special package or custom purchase option you'd like to work out, let us know.

So when your thoughts turn to video, turn your attention to Camera Mart. Whether you're equipping a studio for the future, or producing a program for tomorrow, we've got what you need. The way you need it.

*Plumbicon is a registered trademark of N.V. Phillips.

engineers. We are already in trouble in the digital area. We are starting to spend money on schooling for our own people. We need more maintenance engineers and I don't know where we are going to get them. It is a serious problem; it's going to become *more* serious as the technology grows and becomes more complex. It is *certainly* something that the broadcasters have got to start thinking about. We are already late! Broadcasting today apparently isn't as glamorous to new engineers as the space programs and other things that are going on, and they are passing our business by. Some of them, I think, are missing a good bet.

As far as industrial relations go, I really don't see a big problem there.

Mr. West: Would any of the other panelists like to comment?

Mr. Benson: In the production business, maintenance is as much a problem as in broadcasting. But, as was pointed out in some of the papers on one-inch equipment, there has been a major step forward in reducing the amount of maintenance time and also maintenance costs for materials. For example, it used to take an hour or so to change a head on a quad machine and realign it; now you can do the whole job in 10 to 15 minutes on a helical Type-C format. Not only that, with the one-inch helical machines, you only have to change the head maybe every 1000 to 1500 hours, whereas with quads it's every 350 hours. So, I think our answer in a nutshell to the maintenance problem is that the design engineers will have to come up with continual improvements as they have in taking us from the quad to the one-inch machines. Perhaps going next to the digital recorders will bring about some savings in the same manner.

Mr. Herlihy: I think there is one more comment. I made it during the course of my paper. I think that, as we get more complex electronics and especially digital electronics, the manufacturers do have to start thinking about "self-diagnosis." That is certainly going to cut the amount of time required to troubleshoot these items. I think as they get more complex, we have no choice but to demand that this kind of self-diagnosis be built into the equipment.

Mr. West: Mr. Rainger?

Mr. Rainger: I was going to say something which I hope will help on the maintenance question. As was mentioned earlier, we have a digital sound distribution system which to our delight has a very good fault record; it fails very rarely and it is designed so that it will indicate by lights which printed circuit board has a fault. We have the same thing for standards conversion, where we have a digital standards converter to support the obsolescent 405-line system. Both systems are self-diagnosing to the board. In this case, the question arises of how do you mend the board. The problem we have had to face is that, when it goes wrong so infrequently, the man has forgotten all about what is inside that particular unit, and you have to send it back to base maintenance for repair. This is what we are tending to do at the moment. We have automatic loca-

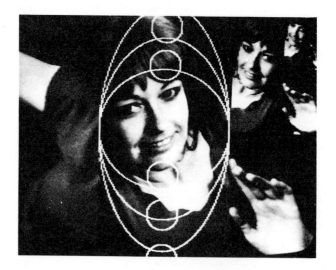

tion to the board and base maintenance for the board itself.

John Lowry, Digital Video Systems: The question of finding maintenance technicians for television stations is a problem. It is, I think, an industry-wide problem from the manufacturers' point of view, too. To find good design engineers today is difficult, to say the least. Is there anything that we can do as a society to help promote the technology we are working with and do anything to get more young engineers into the television business. Certainly the space things are very attractive to people. Television doesn't seem to be attracting people, not in my opinion.

Mr. West: An interesting observation and one that I will not pass to the panel but to the SMPTE organization for whatever they will do with it.

Vern Pointer, the American Broadcasting Company: I think the comments that Blair Benson made earlier are close in line with my observations. We have seen technology make a breakthrough and give us now, in the new one-inch machine, a more cost-effective instrument. We still have maintained our quality; we have not sacrificed anything there; but our operations have become more cost effective. The new one-inch machine uses less tape, is smaller in size, requires less power and has many other features. It now gives us an editing approach and technique which is going to save us a great deal in terms of man-hours. Now, when it comes to the question of a new digital machine somewhere down the line, it is going to have to match all these features as we can't sacrifice any of them. We are not going to go backwards. I think these are the things manufacturers will have to address themselves to.

Mike Frankenburger, Delcom Corporation: I was wondering: In the opinion of the panel, since we are looking at about seven to ten year use of existing machines before the digital VTR is due, would not electronic storage by solid-state memories actually be able to reach the capability to do the same thing by then?

Mr. Benson: I will take a stab at answering that, having just looked into this in the case of bubble memories. If you run some calculations on, for example, the most advanced IBM developments on bubble memories, you will find you can only store even in the highest-capacity units merely a few frames or a few seconds of a television program. So we are a long way's off from a solid-state memory which can handle a commercial-length recording let alone a program-length recording.

Mr. Diermann: The computer peripheral industry is, of course, looking into the ultimate replacement of rotating memories (disk drives) of which we have hundreds and thousands all over the world. A disk drive replacement will require fantastic bubble storage capabilities, and that in television terms is just a few hundred frames. I fully agree with Blair. We will all be very gray by the time that solid-state television program storage comes around.

Mr. West: I have a multiple-part

We hope you'll agree:

Because CMX realizes that editing is the essence of all art, and that to be successful in our work we must appeal to the needs of creativity, our group of engineers and computer programmers work to give video tape editors everywhere an easily understood and widely accepted palette to work from. We have reached that goal with our new keyboard.

CMX delivers.

The appeal of CMX, however, is not just to Art for the sake of Art—far

from it! Aesthetics are only possible in our industry when the cost is right. We also deal with matters such as dependability, expandability, ease of maintenance, and ease of operation during the long nights directors and schedules seem to favor.

Ideas flow.

This new CMX keyboard and interactive display (the first such display of our own design) is an evolutionary improvement. Processor rates for screen update

mean no more waiting. Ideas flow. Dedicated keys for all necessary functions, and the implementation of an active list concept mean re-edit tasks are simple and easily managed.

It's beautiful.

This new television industry standard keyboard is the state of the art you expect from CMX, and what your operating partners expect from engineering.

It's truly beautiful.

the art.

CMX makes dollars and sense.

No obsolescense.
The 340X is today's editing system for professionals, and if history is a guide to the future, CMX is tomorrow's editing tool as well. Obsolescence is not a CMX problem. Micro-processors used in a distributive processing system is not a method likely to suffer obsolescence. As a matter of fact, even our older-designed systems are still in current use—all of them. That's good to know.

Return on investment.
Industrial, educational, and gov-

ernmental usage of video editing has grown as rapidly as top management has appreciated the cost savings of video presentations. The pace has quickened. But the job isn't easy for professional production / post-production managers who must establish the R.O.I. of a complex editing system to the boss who is as interested in throughput per dollar invested as he is any of the aesthetic values CMX brings to bear.

You can bank on it.
In many cases, CMX is the only sys-

tem available which not only does the necessary creative job, but also is the one system with the least overall cost—that's effective! You can bank on it! Smart facility managers realized long ago that the idea of CMX being too expensive was a myth.

We hope you'll agree: The CMX340X makes dollars and sense.

CMX
ORROX

Orrox Corporation, 3303 Scott Boulevard, Santa Clara, California 95050 (408) 988-2000 Los Angeles (213) 980-7927 New York (212) 371-1122 question I would like to put to all the panelists. I think each of us leaving this room ought to have an answer to it, or at least the best possible guess that is presently available. First: Is digital tape recording inevitable? Second: Is it going to happen sometime – presumably as a replacement for analog recording? And third: What is the best guess as to when an operational machine will be ready for purchase at Montreux or the NAB Convention?

Who would like to go first? Charlie Ginsburg?

Mr. Ginsburg: Digital videotape recording for post-production work is inevitable. When people will start to use it is very hard to say. I would say within five years. As to when digital videotape recorders will be in use by broadcasters in general, that's even more difficult to say. I think there has been a consensus expressed here today that, in order to have appeal to broadcasters in general, digital VTRs are going to have to do all the things that the one-inch machines do now and be digital as well.

Mr. Luther: I would also agree that digital recording, at the top end of the market (post production, for example) is inevitable; it's going to happen and probably within five to seven years. I think the continued advance of analog recording, however, will make the generalized introduction of digital recording for all of the uses in broadcasting a very long time off.

Mr. West: Mr. Rainger? What is the European view?

Mr. Rainger: I think I would have to concur about the inevitability of digital recording. I think that's clear. But I think none of us in Europe believes it's going to happen tomorrow. It's a very difficult problem which is going to take a great deal of work to overcome.

Mr. West: One of the comments given to me in the hall and I'll volunteer to you is that digital video recording is chasing a moving target: the moving target of one-inch, which presumably is a far more exciting product than a lot of people thought it was going to be in the first place. The manufacturers are now committed to that, and they presumably feel that that technology will not stand still, so whatever digital developments are demonstrated now have to be compared eventually with an improved analog product. So, I accept the opinion of the experts that digital

television recording is inevitable, they just haven't quite shown me *why* – at this moment. Mr. Rainger?

Mr. Rainger: May I rather *ask* a question? It seems to me that there is fairly broad agreement on the time scale in which these things will come about. We are talking in terms of an evolutionary approach to digital recording, not a revolutionary approach. I would like to ask the question, particularly of Mr. Nasse as to whether, in France, they see digital recording as that far away or whether they hope and believe it to be nearer?

Mr. Nasse: I think the question should not be asked only of a representative of the user's side. I think it's just as much a question which is up to the manufacturers. We agree that, for the European problem in general, the question of adequate standards is more complicated than for the U.S. We basically support the same point of view that digitization is more or less unavoidable and will start on the post-production side of the most sophisticated operations first. Thus, I think it is not possible to give an answer to the question without involving strongly the manufacturers' point of view, which I cannot do.

Mr. West: Are there other questions from the floor that have not yet been touched upon? If not, may I ask each of the panelists if there is a message that they want to get across that they haven't had an opportunity to do?

Mr. Auclair: I would like to make the point that we are finding the reliability and the complexity of digital equipment to be offsetting factors. A problem is that when it goes down, the maintenance engineer has totally forgotten how to maintain it because he hasn't seen it for six months. The answer that the CBC had to come up with about a year ago was to establish a "fireman" squad, on duty 24 hours a day, that travels across Canada back and forth to help people. It is difficult, but we think we will lick the problem.

Mr. Luther: The problem could be solved perhaps by making the equipment less reliable? *[laughter]*

Mr. Rainger: I'd like to mention something which happened almost accidentally in the BBC, where there was this problem exactly. We had a man designing equipment to monitor broadcasting services. They were very complicated digital devices and presented just this sort of maintenance problem. And it became known that

"Harry" designed this equipment, so everybody rang up Harry when it went wrong.

After a time, they began to use a teletype to get answers to their maintenance problems. Now, it occurs to me that the next step along the road is to write a computer program which has diagnostic routines built into it; that seems relatively easy to do. Now anybody can ring up this computer and the computer can print out the answer.

Mr. Diermann: I would like to put a little bit of oil on the water of maintainability of digital equipment. Yes it's true, as Marcel Auclair said, that when the performance of a piece of digital equipment decays, you won't know about it for quite a while because the error correction works harder and harder until all of a sudden it crashes. There is no graceful decay; it decays very, very fast. On the other hand, the service and maintenance of digital equipment – even if you don't have diagnostics – is indeed a great deal easier. We have a piece of digital videodisk recording equipment in our product line, and we definitely notice that it's much easier to bring up the signal system to working condition, because you simply have to ask the question, "Does it go or doesn't it go?" There is nothing in between. So I think we are making a mistake if in general we associate digital equipment with an increased degree of difficulty of maintenance.

Mr. West: That may very well be the last word. I want, on behalf of the audience, to thank the panel, and on behalf of the panel, to thank the audience. At this point, I'd like to turn the microphone over to Fred Remley who has a few closing remarks for the conference. Fred?

Mr. Remley: Thank you, Don. I think we should take an opportunity to acknowledge the effort on the part of the San Francisco section that went into planning this conference. Don Lincoln had to leave early to inspect his transmitter tower, but Carlos Kennedy is still here. Carlos, of course, is responsible for this excellent program and Don for the general arrangements. I think the 820 persons who registered for the conference all agree that it seems much longer than just two days, but at the same time we have learned more than we would learn in any normal two-day period, and that's good. I thank you all. We'll see you in Toronto next year. Good afternoon.